About the Authors

PATRICK RAFTER is Australia's highest-ranked tennis player. He has won two US Opens.

He lives in Bermuda.

LEO SCHLINK is a journalist for the *Herald Sun*. He co-writes a weekly column with Pat, syndicated in News Limited newspapers.

He lives in Melbourne.

ROCKET to the TOP

ROCKET
to the TOP

On the Road with
PAT RAFTER

Patrick Rafter with Leo Schlink

HarperSports
An imprint of HarperCollins*Publishers*

Harper*Sports*

An imprint of HarperCollins*Publishers*

First published in Australia in 1999
by HarperCollins*Publishers* Pty Limited
ACN 009 913 517
A member of HarperCollins*Publishers* (Australia) Pty Limited Group
http://www.harpercollins.com.au

HarperCollins*Publishers*
25 Ryde Road, Pymble, Sydney NSW 2073, Australia
31 View Road, Glenfield, Auckland 10, New Zealand
77–85 Fulham Palace Road, London W6 8JB, United Kingdom
Hazelton Lanes, 55 Avenue Road, Suite 2900, Toronto, Ontario M5R 3L2
and 1995 Markham Road, Scarborough, Ontario M1B 5M8, Canada
10 East 53rd Street, New York NY 10022, USA

National Library of Australia Cataloguing-in-Publication data:

Rafter, Patrick.
Rocket to the top: on the road with Pat Rafter.
ISBN 0 7322 6459 6.
1. Rafter, Patrick. 2. ATP Tour (1999). 3. Tennis players – Australia.
I. Schlink, Leo. II. Title.
796.342092.

Cover photo: Al Bello/Allsport
Back cover photo: Al Bello/Allsport

Printed in Australia by Griffin Press Pty Ltd on 79gsm Bulky Paperback

5 4 3 2 1   99 00 01 02

Acknowledgments

Leo Schlink would like to acknowledge the contributions and assistance of Pat Rafter, Steve, Louise, Geoff and Peter Rafter, News Limited, HarperCollins (Alison, Deonie, Melanie et al.), Wendy Blaxland, Peter Blunden, Phil Gardner, Dan McDonnell, Brian Walsh, Craig Gabriel, Paul Kilderry, Michael Tebbutt, Josh Eagle, John Newcombe, Tony Roche, Mark Waters, George Mimis and the ATP Tour.

CONTENTS

New York
US Open

Brisbane and Townsville
Davis Cup

Europe
Indoor Season

Australia
Getting Fit Again

New York

US OPEN

Relief, followed by utter joy, were
the initial, overwhelming emotions.
Rarely had the words 'game, set,
match Rafter' sounded so sweet. At
the other end of the court stood Mark
Philippoussis, my former doubles
partner and Davis Cup teammate. If I
ever needed evidence of how hard it is to
play a fellow Australian in the final of a Grand
Slam, then this was it.

The scene was the final of the 1998 US Open at Flushing Meadow on
the outskirts of New York. When I won the US Open for the first time 12
months ago, I was surrounded by incredible elation. The win over Greg
Rusedski is still very clear in my mind but it was only when the match
wore into the fourth set that I really began to believe I would win.

Against Mark this year I got on top early in the third set and the match then seemed to roll on very quickly. As satisfied as I was, there was a sense of hollowness to the win. It had been a tough road just to reach the final and, after a tight couple of sets, the match was rapidly approaching its end.

When the match was over, I remember wondering, 'Is this right? Have I really won it again?' It was certainly a different emotion to last year when I really surprised myself — and a lot of other people — by winning the Open.

As is the case with all my friends on the Tour, I made sure I didn't get in Mark's face by overplaying the celebrations on match point. I know how badly he must have wanted to win. He'd worked damned hard to get into the final and played some great tennis.

But it all caught up with him on the last day and I could understand just how bad he must have felt. After walking over to celebrate courtside with my girlfriend Lara Feltham, Mark 'Muddy' Waters (who is the fitness trainer for a lot of the Aussie guys), John Newcombe, Tony Roche and my brothers Steve and Peter, it was time for the presentations.

It was there that the significance of it all began to hit me. It was almost like living a dream. For the second time in a year, I was holding the US Open winner's trophy. Even as a child, I never dared dream I would win it once, let alone twice.

Mark is standing close by with the runner's-up prize. Immediately in front of us is a huge bank of cameras, all pointed at Mark and me. Nearby is Geoff Pollard, president of Tennis Australia. He's a happy man. Mark and I have played in the men's singles final, Sandon Stolle has partnered Czech Cyril Suk to victory in the men's doubles and Jelena Dokic has won the girl's singles.

But amid this scene of peaceful jubilation, a storm is brewing.

Unbeknown to me, Mark and his father, Nick Philippoussis, have taken exception to the fact Rochey sat in my area of the supporters' box. As the Davis Cup coach, Rochey is coach to everybody in the squad.

It was not a slight to Mark, merely confirmation that Rochey had been working with me and several other guys.

I was totally unaware of the furore that was unfolding as I sat quietly in the locker-room while former Australian Davis Cup players Wally Masur, Darren Cahill and John Fitzgerald came in with Rochey and Newk to offer their congratulations.

But it quickly became apparent Mark and his support group had taken offence at the seating arrangements.

I was duly informed of this at the media conference.

Mark had been in before and had accused Rochey of not being neutral.

'To be honest, I expected a lot more, but nothing surprises me,' he said.

When I was told of Mark's remarks, I was pretty annoyed. To me, it wasn't showing Rochey any respect and, if that is the case, I've got a real problem.

Rochey has been the making of me as a player. He's always been there whenever I've needed him and he's done all the work with me. He's not the type of bloke to seek out publicity and he gets a genuine joy out of watching the current batch of Aussies do well.

So to hear one of our own bag Rochey, especially now when I'm on top of the world, is pretty tough to take. Fortunately the disappointment doesn't linger long. There's a big night of partying ahead.

If winning becomes an addictive habit, so does celebrating.

Last year we chose the Park Avenue Sports Bar for the post-tournament party. As the name suggests, there is a large bar-area given over to plenty of televisions, which are generally tuned into sporting events all over the United States.

Out the back is a restaurant. After having a few drinks with just about every Aussie on Manhattan in the front section, we settled down in the restaurant to a fantastic dinner.

In the same way as last year, Newk made a speech, and I replied in kind. Unlike Newk's effort, my speech was short and sharp.

'I've only got six words to say,' I said. 'I dedicate this match to Rochey.' As I looked around the room and saw all the smiling and laughing faces,

I thought about how lucky I am to be in the Australian tennis culture. We're all mates and there's no envy or jealousy there. That is not to say that we don't like beating each other on court; it's just that we really enjoy each other's company.

Needless to say there were plenty of drinks and a stack of laughs. We all end up wearing green napkins on our heads. It is a strange Australian tennis custom which I first experienced after the 1997 US Open win, and I'm unsure of its origin. By the end of the evening everyone was in on the act.

The night seemed to go very quickly and, as it did, I found myself thinking in amazement that I had actually won two Grand Slam singles titles. It was a miracle that I won the first title, let alone came back and won it for a second time.

The hardest thing I experienced that night was actually finishing a beer. No sooner had I worked my way towards the bottom than another beer was thrust into my hand.

I'm not sure what the time was — I know it was late — when Mark Philippoussis and Pat Cash walked in a side door. Apparently it was Cashy's idea to get Mark to come along. It was a gesture from both of them that I really appreciated, given the events of earlier in the day. Mark walked up, we shook hands and chatted before being swamped by photographers and well-wishers.

Mark and I have always been able to talk and I wanted him to know that I didn't appreciate him having a go at Rochey. Tony is the reason I am where I am in the tennis world and, quite apart from that, he's a bloody good friend.

There's no way he would do anything to deliberately hurt or upset anybody, including Mark. I had a long chat with Cashy, who made his views known on the issue in typically honest fashion and we basically agreed to disagree.

As improbable as it seems, the time was perfect to sort out a few issues with a bloke who'd just lost a Grand Slam final.

Mark has been unavailable to play Davis Cup for Australia since the 1997 semi-final against the US in Washington. It was his choice not to represent his country, but we'd love to have him back. It is entirely up to him.

I want to work things out with Mark. His comments about Tony tarnished the win and I don't think Mark stopped to choose his words carefully enough.

The truth of the matter is that Rochey was only doing his job. By attacking him, Mark is not doing himself any favours. By saying what he did, he has hurt a friend. It is not going to help our situation. I want him to come back to the Davis Cup fold, but he's got to feel comfortable about it.

The pity is that Mark is playing great tennis. He's just reached his first major final and, from where I sit, it's only a matter of time until he breaks through and wins at the highest level.

I believe the fact Mark turned up with Cashy — even if it was at 2.30 am — is a significant step forward for everybody.

As we talked, the party raged on. I remember hoisting Rochey, with a little help from my friends, to my shoulders and carrying him around the bar. The bar had been reserved for us all night, but I think even the owners were beginning to tire close to dawn and we eventually left and headed to McDonalds.

It was there, strangely, that some of the memories of the tournament came flooding back.

The best thing about winning again — which has not sunk in yet — is that it has given me a new perspective. To be honest, I didn't think I could win another Grand Slam title and I wasn't sure whether the win last year was a fluke.

But, by winning the US Open for the second time, I've proved to myself that I am capable of doing it for a third time — if everything goes my way. Winning again also shuts up the critics and, to be blunt, it also shuts me up.

The victory last year was a bit of a blur. I was unsure of myself and how I should act or what I should say. As fresh as it is, I think I've appreciated the pleasure of repeating the feat this year. You often hear sports people say they would love to win again just to experience the elation again, knowing that they would enjoy the moment a little more the second time around.

Going into the US Open this year, people were saying I should be worried about burnout because of the number of matches I'd played. The fact is that I need a lot of tennis to play my best, so it is very much a case of the more the better for me.

Coming into Flushing Meadow I'd played 22 matches for 20 wins and two losses, to win tournaments in Toronto, Cincinnati and Long Island. I knew I was fit and that I had done the work. The best part was that I knew I would go the distance, whether I needed three sets or five sets to win.

Looking back on the Open now, I could easily have lost in the first round. I was down two sets to love against Hicham Arazi and he had a huge chance to put me away in the third set, but he didn't take it. I remember telling myself that I had nothing to lose and I started taking some risks.

All of a sudden I was serving for the third set and, once I won that, he didn't get another look in. Unusually for me, I was saying a lot of things to myself out there as I tried to knuckle down. To be honest, Arazi did a few things out there that got me fired up and a little agitated. I didn't appreciate the way he was moving around on my serve on big points. That upset me, along with the way he went on and on about line-calls. In fact, he got me to the stage where I just wanted to beat him up.

I was really happy with my endurance. My record in five-set matches has really improved over the last year or so and I knew I could do whatever it took.

In the end, it was a matter of mentally wearing him down. Even when I was down two sets to love, I never felt out of the match and I was able to win 4–6 4–6 6–3 6–3 6–1.

The next match against Hernan Gumy, who's a good mate from Argentina, went really well as I won 6–4 6–1 6–2. It was a similar story against South African David Nainkin — 6–1 6–1 6–1 — but I knew there would soon be some tough contests.

Goran Ivanisevic, another good mate, duly delivered the test I knew had to come. I won 6–3 6–4 4–6 6–1 and knew I was hitting the ball really well. Then came my doubles partner Jonas Bjorkman. We always have interesting contests and our record against each is about even. I was relieved to survive 6–2 6–3 7–5 to reach the semi-finals.

Standing in my way was Pete Sampras, the world No. 1 and Wimbledon champion. When I won this title last year, Pete was clearly annoyed. He'd won it the previous two years and he made no secret of the fact he wanted it back. I remember going down to Washington for the Davis Cup semi-final a couple of weeks after winning the US Open last year and experiencing just how ferocious Pete was about losing the title.

There was a bit of heat around this match, too, considering I'd beaten Pete in the final at Cincinnati a few weeks previously. I'd been awarded the match on a line-call Pete didn't like and I didn't appreciate the way he'd gone on about what a poor call it had been. I thought Pete had persisted with the line-call issue a little too long.

Now came the opportunity to square off in the semis. Mark Philippoussis played Carlos Moya, the French Open champion in the other semi, and won in four sets to continue his great form.

The match with Pete panned out as expected. There were plenty of winners and a lot of drama.

Pete won the first set, I won the second before he won the third set but injured his left leg in the process. Knowing Sampras was playing with an injury presented a problem. He was hurt, but he was still managing to hit plenty of winners.

Down two sets to one, my first goal was to win the fourth set. I managed that — even though Pete was still moving amazingly well — and squeezed through the fifth set to win 6–7 (8–10) 6–4 2–6 6–4 6–3. Again, I felt the achievement of winning over Pete had been diluted by some of his comments post-match. I don't know of a player who, at some stage of their career, hasn't played with some kind of concern over injury. The fact is that if you're on court, you're fit. You make no excuses — win, lose or draw.

I've always believed in calling it as it is. If the other player is too good, then that's all there is to it. Sure, there are times when you do become injured mid-match but, short of a broken arm or leg, if you're out there and still able to move, and you complete the match, then that's pretty much it.

The irritation of not getting the credit I felt I deserved from Pete was quickly removed by Flip's triumph over Moya, which means it's been a fantastic day for Australian tennis. It is a huge step for the Australian game. It's been 23 years since we last produced two finalists in a Grand Slam and that was at the 1976 Australian Open when Mark Edmondson upset Newk to win the final. Flip's made huge inroads this year. He's got a lot of good people around him now, including his coach Gavin Hopper and Pat Cash. We bumped into each a fair bit out at the courts over the past two weeks or so and stopped for brief chats. We would congratulate each other on our wins and then go about our business. The bottom line was that we both wanted each other to do well.

In a way it was a strange match. We both played well early and then Mark's serve started to let him down. I sensed early in the third set that I was going to win and that's how it panned out.

The most valuable thing I gained, in retrospect, is the confidence to approach every Grand Slam believing I have a chance. Last year I played in seven finals and won only one — the US Open. This year, I've played in six and won six.

That says a lot about the way I'm thinking on court. There is nothing like experience to get you through a tight situation and that's where I can see Mark improving over the next year or so.

For the moment, it's time to get some sleep back at the hotel. It seems like an eternity since I last put my head down for a really solid night's sleep.

Nerves and late matches out at Flushing Meadow do not exactly make for restful nights.

Unfortunately, there's not too much left of this night. But I wouldn't want to trade the good times we've had tonight for anything in the world. As I get to my room, I'm still buzzing with amazement over what's happened.

Soon, however, it will be time to get up — but not before grabbing a few hours sleep — for a photo shoot. It's one of the things I recall doing last year, when I also ended up on *Late Night with David Letterman*.

As satisfying as the past six weeks have been, it is pleasant waking up without having to think about playing a match today. I want to get back to Brisbane as soon as possible to catch up with the rest of the family.

The tennis season is broken into different segments. It starts off with the Australian outdoor summer circuit, then switches to Europe and the US, where corresponding events are run each week until the start of the European clay court season, ending with the French Open. After this comes the grass court season, culminating with Wimbledon, then the US outdoor season which peaks at the US Open. From there, players have the choice of playing in the US, Asia or Europe, where the season ends in late November with a string of indoor tournaments.

After a month's break, it's time for everyone to head to Australia again.

Brisbane and Townsville

DAVIS CUP

Flying home to Australia is always a double-edged sword. The anticipation of catching up with the family again is tempered by the thought of the long flight ahead, but there is nothing like going back to Australia.

I'm going to use the short break to rest and recuperate before the Davis Cup tie against Uzbekistan in Townsville in a fortnight.

Tennis seems to be the only international sport without a substantial rest period at the end of each season. There are enormous commercial opportunities for promoters and that explains why the season stretches from New Year to the end of November. To the uninitiated, a month's break at the end of November might look like time for a vacation. It is nothing of the sort if you want to be ready for the gruelling Australian summer circuit, which begins on New Year's Day and culminates two weeks later at the Australian Open.

I have been deliberately low-key in Brisbane. My priority is to spend time with the family, on the golf course and on the beach.

The toil of playing so many matches in the US has taken its toll. The last thing I want right now is to be running all over town doing interviews or making appearances. I want to preserve my energy for the Davis Cup next week.

Though the Uzbekistanis don't have the longest tennis heritage in the world, there is nothing to say they won't give us a rough time in north Queensland. Davis Cup history is crammed with examples of massive upsets.

Davis Cup is very much in the news. Rochey has quietly threatened to resign as Davis Cup coach over the furore with Mark at the US Open. It is clear Tony has been hurt badly by the controversy and, being such a private individual, is finding it difficult to deal with all the media attention.

From my point of view, it is unwarranted.

Newk has quickly thrown his weight behind Rochey, also taking offence at Flip's remarks. My position is that I'm prepared to join them and not play Davis Cup if either of those guys feel as though they are somehow in the wrong.

Newk is again being dragged back into something he has nothing to do with. He was the meat in the sandwich in Mildura in March, copping it from all quarters when we lost the first round Davis Cup tie to Zimbabwe after Mark chose not to play.

The truth is that he had nothing to do with the whole scenario.

This time Newk's also been accused of sitting in my support box. The truth is that he didn't. He sat on the other side of the railing and was there to interview the people in my box. The whole controversy makes me angry.

They're both champion blokes who have done a lot for Australian tennis.

We can all do without this kind of thing blowing up just when Australian tennis should be on a high.

All of the boys — myself, Mark Woodforde, Todd Woodbridge, Jason Stoltenberg and Lleyton Hewitt — have arrived in Townsville for the Davis Cup.

We're staying at the Hyatt right across the road from a 4900-seat indoor stadium.

The tie has been sold-out well in advance and I'm very excited about playing my first Davis Cup match on Queensland soil.

A lot of family friends are making the trip, even some from Mount Isa.

It will be a big weekend in Australian sport. The Australian Football League Grand Final will be played in Melbourne between Adelaide and North Melbourne.

Because of the interest in the football finals in the southern states, the match times for the tennis are altered. The first day's play will begin at the traditional 11 am, but the doubles on the Saturday won't start until 5 pm, instead of the usual noon start, to avoid clashing with the AFL Grand Final. The reverse singles won't begin on the Sunday until 5 pm, when they would normally start at 11 am. Channel Seven has had a fair influence on these moves, since it is broadcasting both the football and the tennis.

The match court in Townsville is laid over a basketball court used by the National Basketball League club, the Townsville Crocodiles. The arena is affectionately known as the Swamp. Tennis Australia has decided to lay a hardcourt. We're attacking this match as though it is a final.

We lost a similar match to Hungary in Budapest in 1996 and we were blasted in the media as a national disgrace. There's no way we want to risk a similar occurrence, especially since the Uzbekis are virtually unknown outside their own country.

Oleg Ogorodov is a pretty fair player. He's had some good wins in his day and, even though he's ranked over 200 in the world, he plays a bit like Mark Philippoussis. He hits the ball very hard and he's got a good serve.

It is a huge honour for the Uzbekis to play Australia, as they keep on telling us. They are rank underdogs, but they play with tremendous spirit. Jason Stoltenberg is one of those players who sometimes plays too conservatively. Stolts will be the first to tell you that he produces his best tennis when he is aggressive and positive. He showed that at Wimbledon in 1996 when he reached the semi-finals. He played exactly that way against Ogorodov, and I beat Dimitri Tomashevich to put us 2–0 after the first day.

I had been hoping the court would be a touch faster. If anything, it is a fraction slow.

The first day's play went as well as we could expect when there is so much at stake. If we want to vie for the Davis Cup trophy next year, we have to win this weekend. Lleyton is certainly keeping us honest in practice, all the while predicting his beloved Adelaide Crows will win the AFL flag against North tomorrow.

The seafood on display in the Townsville restaurants is just about beyond compare. The North Queensland waters produce a smorgasbord of outstanding seafood and all of the boys are keen to enjoy it.

I take the opportunity to catch up with old friends for a few laughs. This is the first time I've played a professional match at home since about 1992–93. It's a different experience being at home and there are times when I feel the weight of expectation pretty heavily.

We're keen to finish off the tie with a win after spending the afternoon watching Adelaide win the premiership for the second time in as many years.

Lleyton keeps us all amused by jumping all over the room during the second half of the match as the Crows run away with the match.

A few people closely associated with the tie take the chance to go over to Magnetic Island for a day trip.

The pressure switches onto the Woodies, who respond with a straight-sets win over Ogorodov and Tomashevich. The win means we stay up in the World Group, the top level of the Davis Cup competition, which is broken down into inter-zonal competitions under a promotion and relegation system.

In any given year only the 16 nations in the World Group category can win the Davis Cup. Having beaten Uzbekistan means we have a chance of winning the Cup next year for the first time since 1986.

With the pressure off, we arrange a golfing grudge match. The main prize will be decided before we hit off when we toss to decide which team has Stuart Appleby, the professional golfer.

The golf goes well. Stuart is on my team and, naturally enough, our team wins. From there, it's back to the Swamp.

Stolts and I win the reverse singles matches on the Sunday after watching the Brisbane Broncos, my favourite team, beat Canterbury 38–12 for the Australian Rugby League title. Needless to say, it was a big day.

At the end of the tie, Newk makes it clear that Mark Philippoussis is welcome back. So, too, does Stolts, who volunteers to stand down for Flip on the proviso Mark is prepared to put in the hard yards.

The whole team sits down to discuss the issue and, while we're not allowed to talk about it publicly, all of us want the issue sorted out — once and for all. From what we've been told, Geoff Pollard, the Tennis Australia president, plans to talk to Mark at the Grand Slam Cup in Germany.

To be perfectly blunt, the players have had a gutful of the whole thing.

Newk and Rochey don't deserve to have this kind of thing swirling around them and they certainly don't need it.

From my point of view, I feel that Mark is a good guy. I want the whole business at the US Open put behind us so that we can all move ahead.

It's a satisfying feeling to know we're back in the big league and my left knee, which has been bothering me for months, is finally starting to improve.

At the end of the tie, Lleyton got to play a practice set and, as I sat out there watching it, I had the knee manipulated by Vicki Bailey, a masseuse who has done some really good work for me in the past.

As Vicki was working on the knee, it suddenly began to feel a lot freer, so I'm optimistic I'll be fit enough to get through what's left of the season.

After farewelling the family again, I'm heading off to London to spend a few days with Lara before going across to Basel for the Swiss Indoors.

Europe

INDOOR SEASON

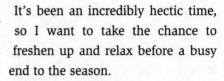

It's been an incredibly hectic time, so I want to take the chance to freshen up and relax before a busy end to the season.

Matthew MacMahon will be coming over from Adelaide to hook up with me for the next three weeks. My brother Geoff will be there as well. I've known Matty for a long time now. He's a good player and we met years ago at a schools' competition and have remained friends ever since.

He's the type of guy I like to have around. We work hard and, if the opportunity is there, we can go out together and relax.

The Swiss Indoors is one of the toughest events in the world. The lowest-ranked player to gain entry into the tournament is No. 35 in the world. My first-round opponent is Daniel Vacek, who's a pretty solid serve-volleyer. He's one of those players who can get hot and cause a lot of damage. And that's exactly what he did against me, although I felt I didn't do myself or the tournament justice. The truth is that I deserved to lose 7–6 (9–7) 7–5. I hadn't done the hard work I normally would have and I paid the penalty. I've been trying to relax and I guess I've overdone it a bit since the Davis Cup.

As the No. 2 player in the world, I'm regularly offered appearance money incentives from tournament directors to play. In return for taking part, I'm expected to help promote the tournament and, in a perfect world, stay in the competition for as long as possible — which every player wants to do anyway.

These payments are known as 'guarantees' and are paid over and above whatever prize money you might win.

The figure sometimes runs into hundreds of thousands of dollars and some players take it regardless of how they've performed. Other guys are different.

I have no hesitation in giving back appearance money if I feel I have not given my best. Hopefully, I can give plenty of value for money. In Lyon last time I handed back my appearance money because I felt I didn't do the tournament justice. I won't say what the figure was, but it was a substantial amount.

I'd just come back from a ten-day holiday and had trained for only three or four days going into the tournament. I lost in the first round. My performance didn't warrant the appearance money, so I had no qualms about giving it back.

After losing to Vacek in the Swiss Open, I quickly came to the realisation that I did not deserve to take the guarantee, so I decided not to take it. I have no regrets about that because I wanted to perform better, not only for myself but also for the tournament.

Tennis gets a bad name for the supposed greed of some of its players.

John McEnroe famously described the players who contested the Grand Slam Cup when it was created in 1990 as 'money whores'. I don't quite see it that way, but there are players out there who are content to take the money and run, irrespective of how they perform. I don't operate like that. There are times when I have lost in the first round and have performed to the best of my ability. In those cases, I have no trouble taking the money because I've performed as well as I could despite the fact my form hasn't been there.

Sometimes it's a bit of the luck of the draw with form, but if you put in 100 per cent, then there's nothing more you can do.

There's no doubt there are some powerful market forces in tennis and there is a handful of players capable of earning big money — especially in Europe and the Middle East.

For all the money, though, you sometimes wonder if the resources could not be better used. The practice facilities in Basel, for example, are possibly the most inadequate in the world. For somebody who wants, and needs, to practise hard and often, having just two courts on which to practise and play is pretty ordinary.

Having said that, every player is in the same boat and I know Pete Sampras and I both lost in the first round and I'm not blaming the number of practice courts for that. But when you consider that I've been having to travel across the Swiss border into Germany just to find a vacant practice court, you can begin to understand what I'm saying.

I'm at the start of a long stretch to the end of the year with tournaments in Vienna, Lyon, Stuttgart, Paris and then Hannover.

Even at this early stage of the last leg, I can safely say I won't be following a schedule like this again. It is far too busy and I'm finding it hard to maintain my enthusiasm at the end of a long and difficult season.

There is a pretty keen incentive at the end of the year, however, and that is the world No. 1 ranking. Pete Sampras has held it for the past five years and if he holds onto it again this season, he will break the record he currently shares with Jimmy Connors.

Sampras is desperate to claim the season-ending ranking and, seemingly, he has the support of Boris Becker, who has given up his wild card invitation into the CA Tennis Trophy in Vienna so that Sampras can play the tournament.

Unusually for Sampras, he has loaded his schedule with more tournaments at the end of the season in the hope of creating a piece of history.

Hopefully I can win one along the way, not only to end the year on a positive note, but to knock him off as No. 1.

The rankings systems can sometimes be difficult to follow. Basically it is a bit like a credit-and-debit system over a 12 month period.

For example, the points I won last year will progressively be taken off my total on the corresponding days this year. And the points I win this year will replace the points I have lost from last year, which leads to a constant reshuffling of the world order.

My knee is still occasionally giving me problems and it is now a matter of constantly monitoring it. All of the tournaments have a strong medical staff and I regularly check out any problems I have with the doctors and physios.

Sampras ends up winning in Vienna. I was reasonably happy with my form, having wins over Byron Black and Magnus Norman before losing in straight sets to Greg Rusedski.

From Vienna, we fly down to Lyon in France for the Grand Prix de Tennis de Lyon. It's one of the classiest events in the world. The tournament is played on indoor carpet and the conditions are fast.

My first-round opponent is American Steve Campbell. I played okay to win 6–2 6–2 and earn another tilt at Hicham Arazi, who's best suited to slower surfaces. I produced some decent tennis against him to win 6–3 6–3 before playing a really ordinary match against South African Wayne Ferreira, who thrashed me 6–4 6–1. My ranking dropped a place from No. 2 as a result, so I'm not too pleased about that.

I get the feeling my body has just about had enough for the year. I'll virtually need to win in Stuttgart in Germany next week, Paris the following week and Hannover after that to have any chance of getting to No. 1.

While I would never say never, I think my chances are fading. At the moment, I'm still leading the points standings going into the ATP Tour World Championships in Hannover, but I've still got a lot of ground to make up on Sampras.

I've had a chat to Boris Becker this week and I've decided to play only one more doubles tournament with Jonas this year because of my knee and hip problems.

What convinced me to cut back the doubles was when Boris said, 'Look Pat, I don't think you should be playing doubles at all these indoor events. The No. 1 ranking is up for grabs, concentrate on singles.'

I've told Jonas and he's agreed to it, so we've already withdrawn from the doubles in Paris and Stuttgart.

I've had hip soreness as a result of a long, grinding year. I play a physical style of game. Serve-volleying really takes a toll on your body and it's difficult to prevent it getting sore, especially at this time of the year.

Across in Asia, Lleyton has forged into the quarter-finals of a tournament to win a bet with Rochey, who had been teasing Lleyton about not reaching a quarter-final in a while. The bet was that Rochey wouldn't have a shave until Lleyton got into the quarters. He did it in Singapore this week and one of the first things he did was to telephone Rochey, ordering him to get the razors out.

Next stop on the neverending tennis circuit is Stuttgart, site of the Eurocard Open. It's another top field, but I've got a first-round bye before I play Swede Magnus Gustafsson. He's a tough player, but the conditions are strongly in my favour. The match goes smoothly as I win 6–1 6–4, but

I WENT INTO THE 1998 US OPEN AS DEFENDING CHAMPION.
NEEDLESS TO SAY, THE PRESSURE WAS IMMENSE.

A TOUGH FIVE-SET
WIN OVER MY RIVAL
PETE SAMPRAS
SET ME UP FOR
A SHOWDOWN IN
THE FINAL
AGAINST FELLOW
AUSSIE MARK
PHILIPPOUSSIS.

CLOSING IT DOWN. ANOTHER BIG POINT IN THE US OPEN FINAL
AGAINST MARK PHILIPPOUSSIS.

I DELIBERATELY TONED DOWN MY VICTORY CELEBRATION IN THE FINAL AS I KNEW HOW BADLY MARK WANTED TO WIN.

THE SMILE SAYS IT ALL: BACK-TO-BACK CHAMPION.

TOP: FIRING A BACKHAND VOLLEY AT THE 1999 AUSTRALIAN OPEN.
BOTTOM: STRETCHING TO MAKE A RETURN.

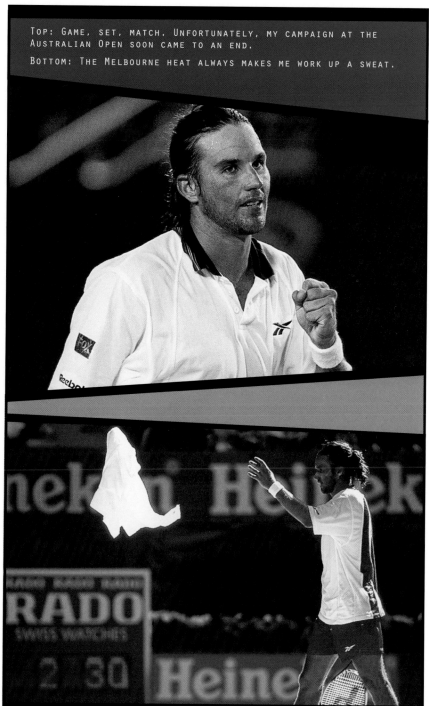

TOP: GAME, SET, MATCH. UNFORTUNATELY, MY CAMPAIGN AT THE AUSTRALIAN OPEN SOON CAME TO AN END.

BOTTOM: THE MELBOURNE HEAT ALWAYS MAKES ME WORK UP A SWEAT.

JACK ATLEY/ALLSPORT

CLIVE BRUNSKILL/ALLSPORT

TOP: KEEPING MY
FANS HAPPY IS
AN IMPORTANT
PART OF LIFE ON
THE ATP TOUR.

LEFT: SENDING
DOWN ANOTHER
BIG SERVE AT
THE AUSTRALIAN
OPEN.

the next round is going to be a lot tougher. I've got Rusedski again and he's building up some really good form.

As he did in Vienna two weeks ago, Rusedski beats me again, although this time it is a very tight match — 6–7 (4–7) 7–6 (7–5) 6–4. I desperately wanted to beat him this time, bearing in mind what was at stake, but it wasn't to be.

Richard Krajicek played outstanding tennis to beat Yevgeny Kafelnikov in the final. I've got one last chance to get to No. 1, but the knee and hip problems are really starting to have an effect on my confidence.

The Open de Paris at the Bercy Stadium will effectively double as my last stand. I beat Nicolas Escude 6–3 6–1 and I finally have my hip problem diagnosed.

It's a relief to know it's nothing serious. The doctors say the pain is caused by degenerative over-use of the lateral meniscus. They fear there might be a small tear in the hip area, but it is nothing I should be overly concerned about.

Rest and good management have been prescribed and, with just this week and the World Championships to get out of the way, I'll soon be able to kick back and get myself right for the start of the Australian summer circuit in January.

It's been a rough year on the body. I'll be having a lot of physiotherapy during the next fortnight. I'm planning to take a short break at home in Bermuda after the Paris Indoors to freshen up before travelling back to Europe for the World Championships.

I'm playing Todd Martin in the next round, but at the moment my thoughts are taken up with an Aussie November custom — the Melbourne Cup at Flemington.

As you can imagine, it's a bit tough to find a form guide in Paris, but a few of the boys are tapping into the latest on the Internet. Most of the guys carry laptop computers these days and there's a fair bit of inter-continental communication.

None of us can claim to be horse-racing experts but we're all hoping an Australian-bred horse or, at the very worst, a New Zealander can win the big race. Unfortunately, we won't be able to sit up and watch it even though we've tracked down an Aussie bar where the race will be shown.

Jezabeel, a Kiwi, wins the Cup and the focus quickly returns to the tournament.

I play another typically tight match against Todd, who's a close mate and a fantastic sportsman. He's a real gentleman on court and there is never any question of him trying to screw me out of points.

On this occasion, he's too good. The scoreline is 5–7 7–6 (7–5) 7–6 (8-6). I don't know it at the time, but it was my final match for the season.

As planned, I head back to Bermuda to get some treatment. My body is fairly beaten up and it's crying out for a rest, which is hardly surprising given that I've played a total of 120 matches on the Tour, plus another three in Davis Cup. I've been around the world, like most of the guys on the Tour, more times than I care to remember and I think I've hit the wall. Most players are in the same boat. And the scary part is that we're midway through November and we need to be going again by Christmas.

There's not much time for a break. Sampras is complaining about the length of the season and he's hardly alone.

Having said all that, there's nothing else I would want to be doing with my life right now. It's a privilege to be living out my dream. This year has been sensational. I've won six tournaments — Chennai, Rosmalen, Toronto, Cincinnati, Long Island and the US Open.

The doubles have been pretty good, too. In partnership with Jonas, I won Indian Wells and Sandon Stolle and I won in Los Angeles.

The doctors in Bermuda advise me to rest, but with the World Championships coming up I'm anxious to get to Hannover. Jonas and I have also qualified for the World Doubles Championships.

But there's a chance that if I keep hammering the knee, and don't rest it, I'll have to have surgery. After a long discussion with my brother Steve, Newk and Rochey and various doctors, I reluctantly decide to abandon plans to play in Hannover.

It's a costly decision in terms of prize money I have forfeited, but it's not the first time this year that I've walked away from money.

I decided not to play the Grand Slam Cup in September in the week after the Davis Cup tie in Townsville because I knew I wanted to rest. As it was, the scheduling made it virtually impossible to play the Grand Slam Cup.

The decision not to travel to Europe for the richest event in tennis meant I effectively left a minimum of $US350 000 on the table. As the US Open champion, I was guaranteed a $US250 000 bonus simply for turning up at the Grand Slam Cup. The money is offered as an incentive to the Grand Slam winners in order to attract the strongest possible field.

The first-round loser's cheque is $US100 000. But my career is not simply about making money. I've been very fortunate in that area. I've earned a lot of money — and paid a lot of tax, too — but I've got to think more now of what's right for me rather than let money become a factor.

Being a large family we had to be sensible with our money. However, my parents, Jim and Jocelyn, always put more money than they could afford on the collection plate at church on Sundays.

It was always drummed into us that, as much as we struggled for money at times, there were always people out there less fortunate than us.

So, to me, money has never been a motivating force. I played in the Grand Slam Cup last year and was runner-up and earned $US1 million for the privilege.

That's a hell of a lot of money.

With the endorsements and sponsorships on offer these days, it's possible to make plenty of money, but I don't think money itself should ever become the reason for playing. When it does, it will be time for me to give it away.

By not playing the World Championships next week, I'll be missing out on more cash, but there's no question what is more important when it comes to a choice between my health and money. I am genuinely sorry that I can't compete in Hannover because it's a tremendous event.

It would have been my last opportunity this year to put some pressure on Pete, but it's not to be. I'm heading off to London and then resting in Bermuda for a few days before planning my trip home to Brisbane.

While I was in London, I caught up with Mark Philippoussis. He's in good spirits and I get the feeling he really wants to be part of the Davis Cup scene again, which is great news for all of us.

Davis Cup is back in the news in Australia with the decision of Peter McNamara and Bob Giltinan to challenge Newk for the Australian captaincy.

While I think Peter and Bob have something to offer, I believe Newk deserves to continue. He and Rochey haven't had a lot of luck in the position, but we all seriously believe we can make a real push for victory next year.

I think Newk is still the best man for the job. He and Tony have brought a lot of professionalism and confidence to the Australian results.

While we've yet to win the Davis Cup again, or perform to the level we'd like, just about everyone has enjoyed their highest ranking since Newk and Rochey came back onto the scene.

Personally, I'd like to see them continue for at least another year and that's not having a go at Peter, who's a tremendous coach, or Bob. It's great for Australian tennis that people feel passionate enough about the Davis Cup captaincy to challenge a bloke like John Newcombe, who is one of the greatest players we've ever had.

As I'm reflecting on my year and pondering what's ahead in the new season, Sampras continues his push for a slice of history, but he runs into a red-hot Jason Stoltenberg in Stockholm. Sampras would have loved to have won in Stockholm and sewn up the year-end ranking, but Stolts showed what a tremendous player he is and was simply too good.

I was really pleased for Stolts simply because he's had a pretty tough year.

He lost a string of tight three-set matches in the middle of the year and went through a really frustrating period when he kept on losing matches in third-set tiebreakers.

The thing about Stolts is that when he plays to his ability, he's a top 10 player. He's been ranked in the top 20 and I think he would be the first to admit he's probably not done his talent justice. The guy can do anything. Perhaps this is the turning point for him.

As I get ready to fly to Australia again, I'm confronting the possibility of surgery on my knee. Even after time off, there is still swelling in the joint and the doctors have said there is significant bruising. Outside of getting the knee right again, my main concern is the Australian Open at Melbourne Park.

The Open is a huge goal for me and I want to be ready for it. For various reasons, I've never done that well at the Australian Open. I'm not sure if it's the expectation or the fact I'm more nervous playing at home.

The Davis Cup tie in Townsville was a step forward for me. Even though I felt the extra pressure, it didn't seem as severe this time. The Australian Open is a slightly different situation. It's the first of the four Grand Slam events — the others being the French Open, Wimbledon and the US Open — of the season and everybody in the field, all 128 of us, is desperate to win it.

It's been 22 years since an Australian won the men's title and that's a drought none of the Aussies wants to see continue. I seriously believe, especially given what's been happening to the Australian game over the past three or four years, that one of us can break through.

The visit to London allowed me to consult a few doctors there about the knee. I've done the same thing in Bermuda. An MRI (magnetic resonance image) was done on the knee in Paris to find out if there was any serious structural damage. Nothing, mercifully, showed up.

I'm tossing up whether I should have an arthroscopy, where the doctors can go in and have a look without causing too much trauma to the knee. In fact, they've told me that if I do have an arthroscopy, I'll be able to walk out of the operating theatre on the same day.

At this stage, I want to continue having the same kind of treatment I had at the Davis Cup in Townsville. It is a pretty critical decision because my whole game revolves around the way I move. But I don't want to get into the middle of next year and find that I really should have had surgery. It's a bit of a waiting game. Do I choose to go in for a nip and tuck, or do I bite the bullet and continue along the same path? The good news is that the hip does not require surgery.

Vicki Bailey will be one of the first people I'll seek out when I get back to Brisbane. Now that my season has finished prematurely, I'll be using the time to getting my body — and mind — right again. They both need to be fresh and healthy by the start of the new year, which is not too far away.

Australia

GETTING FIT
AGAIN

The flight back to Australia has me safe and well. I'm very keen to keep things low-key again. After catching up with the family, it's pretty much a case of heading to the beach, the golf course and the farm at every available opportunity.

After spending so much time on the road this year, the simple pleasure of putting down my roots in one place — home — is something that you never get sick of.

There's no place like Queensland. The natural beauty of the place is incredible and it seems to get better every time I come home.

The cricket season is now in full swing in Australia and it's one of several sports I follow, no matter where I am. I'd love nothing more than to get down to the 'Gabba when the Test match and the one-day internationals are on, but I have to admit the beaches have got a pretty strong hold on me right now.

The ATP Tour continues to wind down into its final phase in Europe.

After losing the final in Paris to Rusedski and then to Stolts, Sampras has to use the World Championships to finish as No. 1 for the year.

He does enough in the end, and without having to win the tournament, and he secures the remarkable achievement of a record sixth season-ending No. 1 ranking. It is truly an incredible feat, but I can't see myself having a celebratory beer for Pete.

While Sampras is a great player, he's not the type of player I would want to spend a lot of time socialising with — or share a beer with. He and I are different characters and we go about our business in different ways. There is nothing wrong with that. He is obsessed with winning and by the No. 1 ranking. I can't say that I'd be so absorbed with a ranking goal that I would cut myself off from the pleasures of life. Pete has admitted that he's missed out on a lot in life to chase his tennis goals.

There are very few people in any kind of profession who'd be prepared to sacrifice so much in order to achieve what Pete's achieved. If nothing else, you've got to admire the guy's sheer discipline and ambition.

The way I'm feeling right now, I can't even look at a tennis racquet, much less want to pick it up and practise.

Doctors in Brisbane have told me that I don't require an arthroscopy, which is a huge relief. I've managed to do a bit of fitness work on the knee this week and I didn't feel any pain. It seems that it is a matter of managing the problem and being aware of what causes it.

I'll be spending plenty of time in the gym trying to strengthen the knee with weights. My plan is to get it as strong as possible in the hope the problem won't flare again. I'm due to play my first tournament in Adelaide in just over a month, so there's not a whole lot of time.

I've put off every commercial and media commitment until after the Australian Open at the end of January to ensure I give myself the best possible chance of doing well on the Australian summer circuit. I've got all the business meetings out of the way this week and I can concentrate on what I need to do to be ready for the new season.

I'm intending to head down to Sydney in the middle of December to work with Tony Roche and Muddy Waters. I'm sure a few of the other players will make the trip and we'll have a training camp. Rochey loves working us hard and I'm sure he's dreamed up a few more lung-busting exercises.

Before I submit myself to his particular brand of torture, I'll head to Adelaide, where I'll play my first tournament of the new year.

The week ends with my win in the sporting category of the People's Choice award. I had to make an acceptance speech and I sounded pretty dorkish. From now on, in case people haven't realised, I've decided to give away my comedy routine and stick to tennis.

I've been considering my tournament schedule for next year and I've decided to cut it back by 25 per cent. Instead of playing 26 singles events, as I did this year, I will go back to something like 18 or 19 tournaments. I'll also cut my doubles tournaments from 19 to about 13 or 14 tournaments.

I wanted to have a couple of really busy and full years to see what I could achieve by giving it everything. I've exceeded my expectations, but now it's important to look at the big picture.

Burnout, both mental and physical, is a very real concern and bound to happen if I keep up my hectic schedule. With the exception of Englishman Tim Henman, who played 29 tournaments this season, I played more matches than any other player in the top 10.

Adding singles and doubles together, my total was 123 matches — plus a few exhibitions or special matches outside the regular Tour which carry no rankings points — so next year I've decided not to meet all my obligations. It will cost me money, but if I started chasing cash I'd be absolutely fried by the end of next season.

My reduced schedule means I won't be going for the ATP Tour bonus pool, which offers money to the leading players based on performance, but that's something I'll have to live with.

The bottom line is not about money. It's about me respecting my health and doing well for as long as I can.

In keeping with my lighter schedule, I've vowed not to pick up a racquet until the day after Christmas and if that means I'll be going into Adelaide and Sydney underdone, then so be it. The Australian Open is my major goal in January. I want to perform there as well as I have overseas and I want to be fresh going in.

If I win Adelaide or Sydney it will be a bonus. I want to win them, make no mistake, but if I'm feeling confident and healthy going into the Australian Open, I'll have achieved my short-term aim.

My decision not to go near a racquet has been overturned in the name of charity. I'm down in Adelaide for John Fitzgerald's Bone Growth Foundation.

These are usually great days. We play golf in the morning at Royal Adelaide — one of the greatest courses in the world — and then have a hit-and-giggle in the evening.

The event raises money for children afflicted with bone growth problems.

Fitzy and Dr Bruce Foster have done some wonderful things for these kids over the years and I'm more than happy to donate my time whenever I can.

The organisers usually round up a field of local celebrities, footballers and netballers to make the occasion a pleasurable affair. This time a stack of Davis Cup players, including Wally Masur, Ken Rosewall and John Alexander, also played.

My tennis was okay, but my golf still needs some work. I managed to sneak into Melbourne for the President's Cup, a high-class event between the US and a composite team made up of Australians, New Zealanders, Japanese, African and South American players.

The tournament was played at Royal Melbourne, another fantastic course, and was won by the International team. While supportive of the International team, I had a special interest in the Australian competitors led by Greg Norman, Craig Parry, Steve Elkington and Stuart Appleby. I got to talk to Greg, as well as Tiger Woods and Phil Mickelson from the

US team, and Parry and Elkington. Hopefully some of their magic can rub off when I play in Jack Newton's golf tournament at Twin Waters over the next couple of days.

Jack was one of Australia's best players until he lost an arm after walking into the propellor of a light plane several years ago. His golf tournaments are always a lot of fun and usually feature a string of sportsmen. It's exactly what I need before the tennis season starts again.

Lara and I go to Noosa for a photoshoot for *Vogue*. I've shot a few commercials in the past, but it's not until you sit back and take notice of everything that goes on during a full photoshoot that you begin to understand how hard these things are.

Lara works hard and I'm certainly more aware of it. We've now done a few shoots together. While it's work for Lara, it's a bit of fun for me. We take the opportunity to kick back for one last week off.

Muddy Waters is coming up to Queensland next week and there won't be anywhere to hide once we start work. I love the routines he has devised for me because I know that if I do the work, I'll get the benefits down the track.

Christmas is now right upon us. As usual, we have a large family get-together. It's a huge operation for Mum and Dad, with nine children and their respective partners. One of the best things about being home for an extended break is being able to spend time at home and eat Mum's cooking.

Unfortunately, the day goes way too quickly. Boxing Day means a lot of different things to different people, but it's generally about rest and recovery. Not for me. I'm on a plane down to Sydney to catch up with Rochey to start hitting for the new year.

Apart from Fitzy's charity, I haven't touched a racquet since losing to Todd Martin in Paris in early November. I know I'll go into the Adelaide and Sydney tournaments searching for form, but at least I feel fresh.

Rochey is typically thorough at the training camp. He loves working us out and pushing us to see how we can improve our games. All too soon, it's time to jump on another flight. This time to Adelaide to get back on the merry-go-round.

Adelaide
AAPT CHAMPIONSHIPS

Sydney
ADIDAS
INTERNATIONAL

Melbourne
AUSTRALIAN OPEN

Brisbane and
Sydney
CHARITY WORK

AUSTRALIA

Adelaide

If there was even the slightest doubt the Australian summer circuit was underway, you only had to be at Adelaide Airport on January 2 to realise the new season was up and running.

Adelaide is where the AAPT Championships, the first serious test of the new season, is played. It is the first of the Australian lead-in events to the Australian Open at Melbourne Park three weeks later. The AAPT Championships is a 32-player event run by Melbourne tournament director Colin Stubs and played on Rebound Ace, a rubberised hardcourt.

Suspecting the local media would be out in force, Stubs organised for my flight to be met on the tarmac by a car which would take me directly to the hotel.

After having my preparation interrupted because of chronic soreness in my troublesome knee, I wanted to slip into Adelaide with a minimum of distraction and get on with the business of practising and playing.

Things would soon heat up, however.

After making the usual round of catching up with all the boys — 'Little Killer' (Paul Kilderry), Josh Eagle, Andrew Florent, Gustavo Kuerten, the 'Woodies' (Todd Woodbridge and Mark Woodforde), Lleyton Hewitt, Thomas Enqvist and all the Swedes — it was down to working hard with Muddy Waters.

I was initially taken aback by the Adelaide heat. An hour into my first hit and my lungs were really feeling the difference.

The good thing was that I had the run behind me and I was reasonably pleased with the way I was hitting the ball, considering I hadn't played a competitive match since Paris in October because of my knee problem.

I've got a couple of days to get myself pumped up. My long-range objective is the Australian Open at Melbourne Park and I'll be doing everything I can in the lead-up tournaments — the AAPT Championships in Adelaide and the Adidas International in Sydney — to get myself in shape. It's been a long time since an Australian has won our Grand Slam event.

Hopefully this can be the year.

But overriding everything else right now — including my preparation — are a couple of startling developments.

The first concerns reigning Australian Open champion Petr Korda returning a positive test to a steroid at Wimbledon last July. Korda tested positive to nandrolone, but he claims he has no knowledge of how it appeared in his system. The most amazing part of the business is that Korda has been given the benefit of the doubt by a panel of drug experts who were appointed by the International Tennis Federation, the highest authority in the sport.

The decision has baffled everybody and there's plenty of talk in the locker-rooms about what has gone on. At this point, the details are sketchy.

Everybody has a theory and there's a fair of bit of anger among the players.

Former world No. 1 and dual Australian Open and French Open champion Jim Courier is really upset. For all his successes, Jim is a champion of the battler. He has always seen himself as part of the wider tennis fraternity, and never above it. He can't see the difference between what Korda has done and what Spaniard Ignacio Truyol did a couple of years ago. Truyol was really struggling to make it as a professional when he tested positive to steroids and narcotics. He was suspended and nobody has seen him since.

Courier has come out and said that he doesn't want Korda to defend his title at Melbourne Park later in the month. Jim says he'll ask for Korda to be ejected from the Australian Open during a special meeting of ATP Tour players in Melbourne in ten days. The meeting has been called by the ATP (Association of Tennis Professionals) which controls the majority of men's tournaments around the world (the ITF, the International Tennis Federation, runs the others). The meeting has been called ostensibly to discuss several administrative issues, but the Korda question is certain to dominate all of our thoughts.

The papers are full of the story and it's really taken the focus away from the start of the season.

The mood in the locker-room is pretty unforgiving.

Jonas Bjorkman, my Swedish doubles partner, has made his feelings very clear from Perth, site of the Hopman Cup, a round-robin tournament which features singles, doubles and mixed doubles under a Davis Cup-style format.

My initial reaction is to give Korda the benefit of the doubt until I can hear from him myself. I've resolved not to say anything publicly until I get all the facts. It's unfair to make accusations when it comes to drugs. Nobody deserves to have their name dragged through the mud unless it's clear-cut they have deliberately taken an illegal substance.

There's always been innuendo about certain players and how they've bulked up over the years. There's the question, too, of how some players continue to play week after week, year after year.

Every player's make-up is different and some have conditions that require medication. They can do that with the permission of the relevant authorities.

I feel that the panel's decision to give Korda a reprieve raises more questions than it answers. Nobody at this stage appears to know what exactly happened at Wimbledon last year. All we know is that Korda had a steroid in his system that he shouldn't have had, and in sufficient quantity to return a positive test.

As such, it remains a mystery how the ITF's independent appeals committee, with its medical and legal expertise, was able to give Korda the benefit of the doubt.

That's all that matters at the moment, ahead of the meeting in Melbourne, but my feelings on drugs remain the same.

If anybody is found to have deliberately taken something illegal to give them a competitive edge, they should be hit really hard and thrown off the Tour. In my opinion, it is nothing more than cheating, and cheating in its worst form.

Within a few days of the controversy erupting, most of the guys have said their piece. A notice went up in the locker-room informing the players that the ATP Tour meeting in Melbourne was compulsory. Failure to attend would attract a fine.

And even though the ATP was at pains to have people understand the meeting had already been convened before Korda's positive test, there was only one thing the players wanted to get clear.

Was Korda within his rights to be still on the Tour or had he been given the benefit of a doubt he shouldn't have had? For the time being, I'm prepared to listen to his explanation but it will have to be good.

My main focus right now is making sure I get off to a good start in Adelaide.

Colin Stubs has assembled a top class field.

Courier has been given a wild card, along with Lleyton who is the defending champion, and there is a stack of outstanding players in town. Wild cards for entry into a tournament are given by tournament directors to players who don't have sufficient points to get into a tournament for various reasons. In Courier's case, he has been a great champion, but his ranking has slipped to a position where he cannot be guaranteed a place in the field. There is no doubt Jim is still a powerful drawcard. In Lleyton's case, he is still in the process of establishing himself and his ranking will not allow him direct entry into the tournament.

The Swedes got to South Australia early and they've obviously acclimatised very quickly. There are seven Aussies in the main draw — Lleyton, myself, Jason Stoltenberg, Scott Draper, Andrew Ilie, Todd Woodbridge and Mark Woodforde.

Hopefully one of us can win it.

'Stubsy' is waiting for replies from Andre Agassi and Pete Sampras to wild card invitations. As much as they would complicate hopes of an Australian victory, their presence would do a lot to boost the tournament. Unfortunately, neither can accept.

Agassi wants to use the Colonial Classic at Kooyong in Melbourne next week as his final lead-up event to the Australian Open. The Colonial Classic is a special event, or exhibition, and guarantees players at least three matches irrespective of whether they win or lose, because it is played under a round-robin format. The AAPT Championships, however, is a regular Tour event, meaning a loss automatically puts you out of the competition.

There is worse news on Sampras.

Reputedly exhausted from the rigours of securing the world No. 1 ranking for the sixth year in a row, Sampras has withdrawn from not only the Colonial Classic, but also the Australian Open.

A lot is being made of Sampras's absence, but there will still be 29 of the top 30 male players in the world at the Open.

The draw has been made for the AAPT Championships and I've got a qualifier, Takeo Suzuki, of Japan.

Qualifiers are often the most dangerous first-round opponents you can have.

Their ranking is not high enough to warrant them direct entry into the main draw, so they have to play in what is virtually a mini-tournament to get into the event. In Suzuki's case, he's had to win three matches in qualifying rounds in Adelaide's sapping heat and I know I'm in for a tough test.

I've been spared the challenge of playing one of the Aussies in the opening round. The last thing I would want is to play an Australian scrapper in the heat. Preferably, you want to meet a European who hasn't been in Australia very long.

Scanning down the draw, the names jump out at you — Michael Chang, Jim Courier, Gustavo Kuerten and Thomas Enqvist, plus all the Aussies except Mark Philippoussis, who's in Perth for the Hopman Cup.

The draw has thrown up some fantastic first-round matches, none more so than that between Lleyton Hewitt and Germany's Nicolas Kiefer, who's now working with Boris Becker's old Australian coach, Bob Brett. They're both young players who have outstanding potential, a great attitude and a hunger to succeed.

My hunch that the Aussies would do well was soon borne out when Scott Draper came back from a set and 1–3 (15–40) down to beat Justin Gimelstob 6–3 in the third before Michael Tebbutt wore down Sebastien Lareau in three sets.

Turning in by far the most impressive performance, however, was Kuerten, who easily defeated Frenchman Jerome Golmard. Guga, as Kuerten is known, has been quite the star with the Adelaide photographers, as much for his unbelievably smooth groundstrokes as for his girlfriend Vanessa Schultz.

I've been given another day to prepare for my match tomorrow night with Suzuki, who's riding a wave of confidence after being given a wild card into the Australian Open by Tennis Australia. He's also happened to knock off Nicklas Kulti, two-time winner of this event, in the final qualifying round. So much for a gentle introduction.

I had good reason to be worried, as it turned out. Suzuki played really well during the first seven games and I could have easily been down a set and in real trouble.

But from 4–3 in the first set, I didn't lose another game, getting out with a 6–3 6–0 win in 53 minutes.

I definitely struggled early and if Takeo had taken his chances, it might have been a different story. I found a way to attack Suzuki's serve and get on a roll. That was the only difference. By moving closer in on my returns, I was able to find an edge. That's how marginal the difference between success and failure can be.

But I am pleased to have survived. It had been a long time between matches and there is always a sense of uncertainty and anxiety. Rankings in this situation are meaningless.

The most satisfying aspect of the whole match was the fact I got through without feeling any pain in my knee. That was very promising, but I can't let up on trying to strengthen it.

Having decided to opt out of surgery, I'm committed to a maintenance program and that's where Muddy Waters comes in. As I've said, Muddy is a fitness trainer employed by Tennis Australia, and he works with several Aussie guys. He knows what I should do and how much I should do.

I'll be in the gym tomorrow as part of the program to make the knee stronger.

Memorial Drive is one of the oldest venues on the Tour and has claimed more than its fair share of victims over the years. Today has been no exception.

Slava Dosedel, of the Czech Republic, is one of the few instinctive serve-volleyers in the world and he's shown just how well he's playing by eliminating Jim Courier 7–5 6–3.

Jim is struggling at the moment to get his game going after a long battle with tendinitis in his right arm. But he's still a very dangerous player. Given Courier's current ranking of 77th in the world, it's easy for people to forget he has four major titles to his name. But there's no way any of the players is going to write him off. He's still got a lot left in the tank and I'm sure he'll be back.

Todd Woodbridge also had a tough day, losing 6–4 6–2 to Italian veteran Gianluca Pozzi in blistering heat.

'Teddy' told the media after the match he was still affected by the death of Renay Appleby — wife of the top Australian golfer Stuart Appleby — in a car accident in London in July. Todd and his wife Natasha were pallbearers at Renay's funeral and Todd now wears a goatee in honour of Renay.

It's been a difficult time for a lot of people since the accident.

Renay's death was a huge shock to Teddy and Natasha and I can understand how shaken they are.

'I've been keeping my emotions in and I'm still doing that,' Todd said. 'The importance of tennis in relation to some other aspects of my life has changed.

'When you get older, and now that I'm married, other things become important.

'It's a process of growing.'

The Applebys have a home in Florida, where a lot of the Aussies live.

Overseas bases for Australian sportspeople are now very much in vogue. It is too tiring to travel back to Australia all the time in between tournaments and there is nothing worse than having to travel from hotel to hotel. It is far easier and a lot more comfortable to have our own homes overseas, although it is a little expensive.

Andrew Ilie had a match he would prefer to forget, losing 6–2 6–1 to Czech Jiri Novak, while Mark Draper couldn't emulate his brother's win, falling 6–2 6–0 to German Oliver Gross.

The presence of Zimbabwean Davis Cup star Byron Black at the AAPT Championships has ensured there is growing interest in the first-round Davis Cup match between Australia and Zimbabwe in Harare in April.

'Blacky' helped nail the Aussies in Mildura last year in a surprise 3–2 win and he's obviously hoping to do the same when we travel to Zimbabwe in a couple of months. Hopefully this time we'll be able to beat him, especially since Mark Philippoussis is back after making himself available to play for Australia.

I have other mountains to climb right now and, despite my hopes of a good week in Adelaide, I'm shown the door by Dosedel, who's turning the business of upsetting higher-ranked opponents into an art form.

I thought I was primed to improve on my first-round match, but I went backwards. Dosedel cleaned me up 7–5 6–4 and now I've got to pull my finger out and really try to get my court movement going in Sydney. I need to be able to move well, especially into and around the net, to play my best tennis.

Time is running out to be ready for the Australian Open at Melbourne Park in ten days' time and I'm concerned about my motivation.

I'm probably not in the best shape I've ever been in because I've been trying to protect my knee, so I've got a lot of work to do. The simple fact is that I need to move well to play well.

I'm not someone who feeds their ego with bullshit. I'm the type of player who gets confidence out of winning matches and practising really hard. When you've done the work, you can go in and play a free-flowing game and that really takes away the pressure.

I tend to play my best when I'm getting a lot of matches, as I have in tournaments leading into the US Open over the past few years.

The biggest worry about losing in the second round in Adelaide is that I've got only one more chance to get it right in Sydney and that will not be easy.

I head straight for the practice courts to try and find some rhythm.

Not for the first time, media questioning has focused on my ability to handle public expectations. It's great to have the public support I have, but there are times when it does become tough. There are occasions when you don't want to deal with people. It's difficult to handle things sometimes when people come up at dinner when I'm with Lara or my family and want autographs. It tends to happen a lot in Australia. At the end of the day, though, it's a trade-off and a very small sacrifice.

When it gets too much I can always have room service!

Lleyton Hewitt kept Australian hopes alive with a three-set win over Jiri Novak.

Lleyton plays Dosedel next. For some strange reason the crowd seems to be on Lleyton's case this year. They often seem to barrack for his opponent, despite the fact that Lleyton is an Adelaide boy. It's probably the tall poppy syndrome kicking in early, which is a real shame, especially since Lleyton is so young and playing in his home town, where he was born and has lived all his life.

Scotty Draper beat Michael Tebbutt to reach the quarter-finals and Thomas Enqvist just keeps getting better with a straight sets win over Dominik Hrbaty.

I'm now headed for Sydney, White City and the practice court. In the meantime, Lleyton continues to grab the headlines. He's nailed Dosedel in three sets and is into the semi-finals. He's in good company.

Lleyton will play Stolts, whom he beat in last season's final. Stoltenberg got through with a great 6–3 6–2 win over Byron Black, partial revenge for what happened in Mildura. When Stolts plays as aggressively as he did against Black in the quarter-finals, it's easy to understand why he got to the Wimbledon semi-final a couple of years ago.

Sydney

ADIDAS INTERNATIONAL

Sydney is a zoo. There are cameras and people everywhere. White City is hosting the Adidas International — the old New South Wales Open — for the last time. From next year the tournament will be played at Homebush Bay at the Sydney Olympic Games site.

White City has been a great venue over the years and I have reason to rate it favourably. It was here two years ago that my career turned around in a Davis Cup match against Cedric Pioline. I came back from two sets down to win in five sets and I think I really learned to believe in myself that day. I attributed my first US Open win to the confidence and faith in myself I had when I was playing Pioline. I could do with some of that over the next three weeks and it is reassuring to be on familiar ground — especially in a place where you have overcome the odds to succeed.

Across the country, Australians are doing well. Mark Philippoussis and Jelena Dokic have won the Hopman Cup for the host nation for the first time and, in Adelaide, Lleyton Hewitt has reached the final, where he will play Thomas Enqvist, who is quietly firming as a dark horse for the Australian Open.

I've filled the hours working flat out in Sydney with Tony Roche and Muddy Waters, trying to improving my movement. Time really is running out for me if I want to get my game cranked up for the Australian Open.

Looking back on the match with Suzuki, I thought I played well, but I was definitely half a step slow against Dosedel. If I'm in similar shape in Melbourne, I won't last for long.

The Korda drugs controversy continues to simmer.

The calls for his ejection from the Australian Open seem to grow louder by the day. By all reports, the players, officials and media who have had a chance to speak to him at the Qatar Open in Doha have been convinced of his innocence.

I'm reluctant to jump to any judgement so, as uncomfortable as it is right now, I'm sitting on the fence until Korda has had the chance to stand up in front of the players and give his side of the story. I want to hear Petr explain how a steroid ended up in his system.

And, for his sake, I'm hoping he's got a bloody good explanation because I'm totally opposed to drug-taking in any form.

I wake to another day of practice as the Adidas International gets underway and my summer takes another interesting turn. My first-round opponent in Sydney is none other than the resident Australian giant-killer Lleyton Hewitt.

There are just no easy matches out there. Lleyton proved his form and development by taking Enqvist to three sets in 41°C heat in the Adelaide final. Now it's my turn to have a crack at the young bloke.

Sydney is now in the grip of a searing heatwave. It's 40°C at White City and I'm next door at Sydney Grammar School, taking part in the ATP Tour's Fan Fest, which is a fun way of helping kids get close to the players and, at the same time, learn a bit more about tennis and the ATP Tour through games and competitions. It's all part of the deal of being an ATP Tour player, although I must say some put more effort into it than others, who are not so generous and tend to bludge on the rest. Thankfully, they're in the minority.

The way I look at it is that we should all be available up to a point and do our bit to promote the game.

The popularity of the exercise is borne out by the 500 spectators who turned up for autographs and a chat about techniques and life on the Tour.

In many ways, it's a good way to get a grip on things.

The media is running plenty of stories on my match with Lleyton.

Asked how it felt to play against Hewitt, I replied: 'Good. The worst thing is that I'm going to lose.' What I really have, though, is the opportunity to win a few matches this week but I know I'm going to have to work for it.

My form is slowly coming back together. Rochey's got me working hard and it's been good to spend time with Lara in her home town. It's the closest thing for me to being at home on the road.

White City's centre court was packed out. The last time I saw it like this was against Pioline. Unfortunately for me, there was no golden ending to this match.

I ended up losing 7–6 (7–1) 6–1 before a crowd of 7000. Lleyton played great tennis. And it was another strange match for me.

I was really happy with my fitness and the way I moved — which is something — but I remember feeling odd out on court.

My concentration slipped. I'd play a shot and ask myself why I'd done it. I kept on questioning every shot I played and I missed a lot of the volleys I would normally make. I guess it was pressure. When I'm playing at my best, my game is based on instinct. It just flows.

Not for the first time, I'm wondering about my preparation.

Perhaps I've been too accessible. It's hard to smile all of the time. I think I need to spend a bit of time by myself. I know a couple of quiet spots in Melbourne and that's where I'll head. I feel very under-prepared at the moment.

Having said that, Lleyton deserved to win.

As tends to happen at this time of the season when the guys are feeling their way back into it, the form holds up pretty well.

So it was hardly surprising to see Hewitt beat Nicolas Kiefer for the second time in as many matches. The bookies, ever conservative, slashed Lleyton's price from 200/1 to 40/1 for the Australian Open. Perhaps they knew something.

Jason Stoltenberg, a semi-finalist in Adelaide, upstaged Richard Krajicek in straight sets.

Richard Fromberg is in the wars, however. 'Frommy' has been forced out of the Open with a wrist injury sustained in falling from a bike while riding to the Melbourne Park National Tennis Centre. Apparently the straps from Richard's racquet bag became entangled in the wheels, leading to a heavy crash.

Melbourne

AUSTRALIAN OPEN

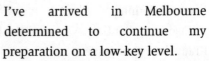

I've arrived in Melbourne determined to continue my preparation on a low-key level.

I've booked into the Crown Towers at Southbank, which sits on the River Yarra and is perfectly situated to Melbourne Park and the city itself.

Before I head off to practise, in quest of the form and confidence that seems to have deserted me, I have a more pressing engagement.

My left wrist has stayed sore and swollen after a fall during my match with Lleyton in Sydney. Fortunately, it is not my right wrist, but it's still enough of a distraction for me to consult a doctor.

A MRI (magnetic resonance image) scan shows there is no bone damage, but there is still a measure of swelling. I'll just have to nurse it a little.

The media is currently preoccupied with Korda's arrival in Melbourne for the Colonial Classic and there is no sign of the controversy letting up.

If there is a benefit from the whole incident it's that I've been allowed to practise in peace. Not that uninvited guests are welcome at the Capital, the first-class golf course and sporting facility owned by Lloyd Williams, the proprietor of Crown Casino.

It is there each day that, with the help of Paul Kilderry, Josh Eagle, Michael Tebbutt and a few good mates, I've been able to put in the hard yards without having to worry about doing interviews or posing for photographs.

I'm keen to get another match under my belt and the only avenue is the Colonial Classic, the special event being played at Kooyong at the same time as the Adidas International. But first I have to be released from the Adidas. My brother Steve is currently locked in negotiations with the tournament director of the Adidas International, Barry Masters, and the tournament director of the Colonial Classic, Colin Stubs.

Barry Masters generously gives his approval and Stubsy sets up a match on the Saturday against Mikael Tillstrom. In the meantime, Rochey and the boys have been working me hard at the Capital.

Mark Philippoussis, the architect of the Hopman Cup triumph, is now 7/1 favourite for the Australian Open. Considering my form, I'm surprisingly installed at 8/1, along with Andre Agassi.

Philippoussis bears out the rating with a tight win over Tim Henman in the first phase of the Colonial. More ominously, Thomas Enqvist knocks off Goran Ivanisevic, Agassi hammers Korda and Michael Chang downs Yevgeny Kafelnikov 7–5 in the third.

The draw is made for the Open. I've got German Oliver Gross in the first round. I studiously avoid looking any further into the draw than my next match, yet I can't help being told that I'm destined for a third-round appointment with Enqvist.

John Newcombe, Rochey and Muddy have been working overtime on the mental side of my game. Slowly but surely it's coming together.

Hewitt and Stoltenberg lose to Todd Martin and Thomas Muster respectively in Sydney but the White City crowd is thrilled by Steffi Graf's three-set semi-final win over Venus Williams. Sydney is one of the few tournaments in the world, outside of the Grand Slams, to combine the men's and women's tournaments. It makes for a lot of jostling for practice courts, but the atmosphere is certainly different.

Details of an interview with Mark Philippoussis in American magazine *GQ* finally surface in Australia and the focus is on my relationship with Flip in the wake of the 1998 Davis Cup dispute.

Whatever problems Mark and I had over him not being available for the Davis Cup are now dead and buried and that much is made clear in the latest article.

I think very few people understood how intricate the whole situation was. Mark is different, but he's a good guy. I used to play doubles with him and we still get along well.

We had a chat last year trying to resolve issues, and it has been heartening watching him getting along with all the other Davis Cup guys, as well as Newk and Rochey.

I'm now desperate to play. My motivation to get out on court is returning quickly. I've always found that a loss is a pretty good way to get motivated.

There's nothing like a good kick up the backside, which we all need from time to time.

The No. 1 ranking is also being talked about — again — with Pete's absence. Since I've been No. 2, the next logical goal has to be No. 1. It doesn't automatically follow that just because I've been No. 2, I'll reach No. 1. Nevertheless I want to give it my best shot and see what happens.

With Sampras staying in the States, the door has certainly opened, not just for myself, but for Marcelo Rios, Alex Corretja, Carlos Moya and Andre Agassi.

Looking at that group of players, the first thing that strikes you is how different we all are, but I can guarantee you there is a common attitude. None of us will place any more emphasis on the ranking system than usual.

I've always said that if you play well the ranking will take care of itself.

At the moment it is pointless talking about the ranking, since I'm not even sure that I'm playing well. If I do well at the Australian Open, that will be reflected in the rankings.

I'd love to win the Australian Open. It is the tournament I want to win more than any other, along with the Davis Cup, now that I've actually won at Grand Slam level. To do that, I'm going to need to get my arse into gear. I've been protecting the knee a bit, but the good thing about Adelaide and Sydney is that I've been able to get through without any problems.

The Australian Open absentee list threatens to grow a little longer with Ivanisevic withdrawing from the Colonial with a sore back. Philippoussis continues to impress, this time upstaging Michael Chang 6-7 (2-7) 7-5 6-3.

Tillstrom, stepping in for Ivanisevic, comfortably beat Henman 7-5 6-1 and Kafelnikov ground his way to a three-set win over Korda.

I'm due to play at noon tomorrow and have a few butterflies, which is a good sign.

It's going to be a big day. First I've got Tillstrom and then comes the much anticipated player meeting at the Hyatt Hotel.

The first set could not have panned out much better. It was just the kind of match I needed, in pretty warm conditions. I moved well and won the first set 6-1.

I had a couple of chances to lead 2–0 in the second set before Tillstrom levelled the match by winning it 6–2. I ended up winning 7–5 in the third and felt as though a little weight had shifted off my shoulders.

Tillstrom might be ranked 86th in the world, but he is clearly a much better player than his ranking would indicate. And even though it was only an exhibition match, the important thing was that I had actually won a match again. Exhibition matches are invaluable in providing opportunities to work on various aspects of your game.

I've done as much as I can to minimise outside influences in the company of my brothers, Peter and Geoff, as well as my mates Little Killer, Josh and Tebs. We've been doing three-hour workouts and then rewarding ourselves with rounds of golf, sometimes at Kingston Heath and Huntingdale, which are among the premier courses in Melbourne.

There's no time for golf today. After the match with Tillstrom, it's back to the Capital and then off to the player meeting at the Hyatt.

Enqvist continued his outstanding form by easily beating Mark Philippoussis in the Colonial Classic final. The Swede will go into the Australian Open unseeded, which spells danger for everybody, myself included.

Every tournament has a seeding system. The highest-ranked player is seeded No. 1 and has their name placed at the top of the draw. At most tournaments, there are eight players seeded. Part of the reason for seeding is to prevent the highest-ranked players playing each other early in the tournament. If there weren't seeds it would be possible for the world No. 1 to play the world No. 2 in the first round of a tournament. At the Australian Open, which is one of four Grand Slam events along with the French Open, Wimbledon and the US Open, a total of 16 players are seeded.

The long-awaited player meeting is a farce.

Everybody, including Korda, turned up, but there was nothing in the way of an explanation from Petr.

Instead we got virtually a lecture from a group of drug experts on the drugs detection procedures, the penalties and the philosophy.

Korda didn't say a word.

What I would have really liked was for him to have told us how the steroid got in his body.

Jim Courier went in hard at the meeting, demanding Korda be expelled from the Australian Open and kicked off the Tour pending an investigation. The mood of the players was adequately captured with the standing ovation he received.

I ended up sneaking out the backdoor before the meeting ended. I believe it rambled on for four hours or so. There was no way I was going to stay there that long, simply because the people concerned were avoiding the issue. I walked as soon as it became obvious we weren't going to get any straight answers, right behind Goran Ivanisevic. The fact that a Grand Slam champion returned a positive test at Wimbledon — the biggest and most important tournament in the world — and has not been penalised is killing the image of tennis.

If athletes return a positive swab in other sports, they are kicked out straight away.

It should be the same in tennis. Unfortunately, in this case, tennis's reputation has been dragged through the mud and, as much as the officials want to argue it has inflicted no damage on the other players, I think otherwise. The result of a month of discussion is that Korda, despite a steroid being found in his system, will have the opportunity to defend his title.

Tomorrow is the last chance to rest and relax. From Monday, there will be nowhere to hide.

The opening day is predictably demanding. I get through against Gross and Flip takes care of Geoff Grant. The crowd was fantastic and I feel my form is slowly returning. The noise on court was deafening at times. At one stage I looked up into the stands and saw Melbourne's —

and probably Australia's — leading jockey Damien Oliver revving everybody up.

But there are a couple of storms brewing.

Philippoussis's coach and former Wimbledon champion Pat Cash has let fly in an interview on *Today Tonight*, a current affairs program shown by the Open's host broadcaster, Channel Seven.

Among other things, Cash said John Newcombe had been unfair to Mark, bringing up the claim again that Newk and Rochey had sided with me during the US Open final by sitting in my support box.

Given Cash's relationship with Newk, which became strained in 1983, it was not surprising that he would unleash such an outburst.

But it was still disappointing to hear Cashy have a go at another Australian champion, especially with the tournament just starting.

'I think it takes a lot of guts for a guy like Mark to go to Zimbabwe and to be sitting down on court with a captain who clearly doesn't respect him and whom he doesn't respect,' Cash said in an attack that he first mounted in the middle of last year in the wake of the 3–2 loss to Zimbabwe in Mildura.

Flip, to his credit, moved to defuse the controversy by refusing to buy into it and, within a couple of days, Cashy and Newk had met and chatted about the issue, though not before a lot of other people were dragged into it, including Victorian Premier Jeff Kennett, who condemned Cashy for the timing of his attack.

My new-issue Reebok shirts have attracted the attention of the officials and they've asked to take one away to examine it. Reebok has been my long-term clothing and shoe sponsor and they routinely make new releases each year.

But the officials in the Australian Open have a problem with the collar, or lack of one. However, I'm confident the issue will be resolved.

The shirts are different and very Australian. They've been described as a bit of a beach look.

Eventually, I'm given approval to continue wearing the gear. The collars are pretty small, comparatively, but there is a collar there.

It's been a good first day for the Aussies. Apart from myself and Flip, Mark Woodforde, Andrew Ilie and Sandon Stolle have got through.

But Todd Woodbridge, Toby Mitchell, Wayne Arthurs and Joe Sirianni were knocked out. Unfortunately for Wayne and Joe, they both lost in five sets, which is especially tough given that they are Victorian wild cards playing at home in front of their friends and families.

Ivanisevic and world No. 2 Marcelo Rios have withdrawn with back injuries.

Goran headed straight home, saying it was too much to hang around the locker-room and watch the other guys play when he couldn't take part, proving once again that injury is the professional athlete's worst nightmare.

I've got Mark Woodforde in the second round and I know exactly how crafty Pecker can be. There's no way I can take anything for granted in this match.

He's won two tournaments on Rebound Ace in his time and he's been an Australian Open semi-finalist. Mark beat me in the first round at Wimbledon four years ago and I don't want to let this one slip.

Pecker is not quite at his top and I played very well to get through 6–2 6-4 6-4. In fact, it's the best I've played since the Paris Indoors last year.

The most pleasing aspect was that I moved well. And it was especially good to back up the win over Gross. Now comes Enqvist. It's a huge match for both of us. The winner will probably play Mark Philippoussis in the fourth round after Flip won a magnificent five-setter — 7–5 in the fifth — against Michael Chang in almost four hours.

Nobody could possibly doubt that Mark has everything that's needed to win a major. He was fantastic against Chang.

Mark Woodforde tells the media that if I can beat Enqvist then I will have reached the standard needed to win the Open. He's probably right because Enqvist is flying right now. I'll try and play my style of game against Thomas and attempt to put a lot of pressure on him.

Korda, meanwhile, has surged into the third round.

The drugs issue continues to sour proceedings. The atmosphere in the locker-room has changed and it's not hard to see why.

I've put my name to a media campaign that hopefully will lead to the removal of drugs from sport.

Greg Norman, Ian Thorpe and Australia's Olympic gold medal-winning rowing team, the Oarsome Foursome, have also signed a statement which describes drug cheating as the ultimate sporting crime. It's designed to send a message to athletes ahead of the Olympic Games in Sydney next year. The Australian Olympic Committee has decided to commit $1 million to help educate athletes about drugs and rehabilitate those who succumb to performance-enhancing substances.

Record crowds continue to flock into Melbourne Park as Lleyton Hewitt, Sandon Stolle and Jason Stoltenberg bow out, leaving only myself, Flip and Andrew Ilie in contention.

The match with Enqvist has been hyped to death — as I expected.

Unfortunately I wasn't about to pull a rabbit out of the hat and reach the fourth round, where I would have played Flip.

Enqvist won 6–4 4–6 6–4 6–4 in two hours and 33 minutes. I didn't do a lot wrong out there. Thomas was simply too strong and too good.

I did OK under the circumstances. Thomas is playing exceptional tennis at the moment and he put me under enormous pressure. His forehand is rightly regarded as one of the most potent weapons in international tennis. But his serve — first and second — is equally solid.

The second serve is where I like to attack players and try and break them down, but Enqvist gave me no chance and, being such a good returner, he made me pay on my serve. Despite suggestions the conditions had quickened enough to suit players such as myself, Philippoussis and Tim Henman, the baseliners still have the edge at Melbourne Park. History shows players who generally play from the baseline have had more success on Melbourne Park's Rebound Ace than the serve-volleyers.

The reality has hit that I won't be taking home the Australian Open singles title, but I have plucked some positives out of the experience. It has been another learning curve for me.

I haven't always relished the pressure of playing at home, but I adapted better this year. Managing to keep out of public view during much of my time in Melbourne was a good thing.

I found the privacy I needed to practise and relax, playing quite a few rounds of golf at the Capital — a diversion which really helped me.

Unfortunately I wasn't able to capitalise on it. But the bonus, despite being out of contention in the singles, is that I'm feeling healthy and positive about my game.

The knee has not been a problem, but I have taken the step of slashing the number of tournaments I'm playing from 26 to 19. The top-ranked players have to play a certain number of tournaments each season, but once you reach that minimum figure, it is up to you how many more you play. My move to play fewer events is inspired by the need to protect myself physically as much as mentally. The overall objective is to be playing good tennis towards the end of the year and, most importantly, to retain my sanity.

A few of us head off tonight to watch Men at Work at the Mercury Lounge at the Crown Casino. I'm still in the doubles with Jonas, but I needed to get out with Little Killer, my brother Geoff, Josh Eagle, Andrew Florent and a few of the boys.

With my lighter schedule, Josh and I take advantage of a fantastic invitation from Crown to play down at Cape Schank golf course at the bottom of the Mornington Peninsula south of Melbourne. It's an awesome course with incredible scenery, but the best part is travelling to and from the course by helicopter.

Enqvist has now won 11 matches in a row after claiming titles in Adelaide and Kooyong. He now faces Philippoussis, who really is showing all the signs that he is on the brink of breaking through at Grand Slam level. He beat Jan Kroslak 3–6 6–3 6–4 6–1 after making a sluggish start, which I'm sure was a legacy of his long match against Chang.

Flip's off-court habits have improved, too. He's cut out the junk food and has got a lot fitter working under Gavin Hopper and Pat Cash, who have taken Mark's mental approach to a new level.

The nominations are out for the Australian of the Year and I've been included, along with Australia's cricket captain Mark Taylor and world 500cc motorcycle champion Mick Doohan, another Queenslander. Just being nominated is an honour.

The shocks continue, meanwhile, at Melbourne Park, where Andre Agassi's form dries up and he loses a strange match to fellow American Vince Spadea.

There are times when Andre looks like he's ready to win another major, but this wasn't one of those days.

Worse still for Australia, Thomas Enqvist eliminates Mark Philippoussis after a tremendous centre court clash. Flip fought desperately right to the end, but Enqvist was able to regain the initiative when it mattered most and win in front of a crowd which roared itself hoarse attempting to lift Mark to victory.

Enqvist had pockets of support from the always vocal Swedish tourists — and some of the local Swedephiles — and held his nerve long enough to reach the quarter-finals.

He is now the overwhelming favourite to win his first Grand Slam singles title.

If he's successful, nobody is going to begrudge Thomas the achievement.

Enqvist's latest victim becomes Marc Rosset, the luckiest man in tennis since he chose to change his booking in New York last year and not catch Swissair Flight 111 which later crashed with no survivors off Nova Scotia. Enqvist beat Rosset in straight sets. Rosset was foot-faulted nine times in the match, an unusually high statistic for a player at this level.

Ecuadorian Nicolas Lapentti continues to win a string of new fans, mostly female, with his performances and few come better than his 7–6 (7–4) 6–7 (6–8) 6–2 0–6 8–6 win over Karol Kucera. As commanding as Lapentti was on court, television viewers spent a lot of time digesting pictures of Anna Kournikova and Gustavo Kuerten urging the South American to victory.

The strength of Lapentti's friendship with Kuerten was amply displayed when Kuerten consented to Lapentti's request to pull out of the doubles quarter-final because of exhaustion. Jonas and I aren't too bothered about it, either, since it pushes us directly into the semi-finals, courtesy of the walkover.

It is precisely the type of luck you need at a Slam. It could prove to be critical in the end.

Lapentti was duly eliminated by the rampant Enqvist 6–3 7–5 6–1 in the semis who will now play either Yevgeny Kafelnikov or Tommy Haas — whoever wins — in the final.

Jonas and I offer a silent vote of thanks to Lapentti for withdrawing from the doubles after we beat the Woodies 3–6 4–6 6–2 6–2 8–6 on Court One to reach our first major final as a team. Jonas has been there before, but this is my first time.

It was an incredible feeling just to make the final, where we'll play top seeds Mahesh Bhupathi and Leander Paes of India. It is a great opportunity and we're both really pumped for it.

The women's tournament has suddenly surged to the fore with Lindsay Davenport and Martina Hingis making comments during media conferences about French teenager Amélie Mauresmo. The media is whipped into a lather of condemnation and counter-claim as Mauresmo reacts to comments basically accusing her of being half a man. It seems Mauresmo's sexuality is an issue for some players on the women's Tour. Hardly the ideal preparation for a 19-year-old playing her first major final against the defending champion, who just happens to be Hingis.

I've tipped Enqvist to win the men's singles, simply because I think it's his time. But he has to continue as he is doing and remember how he got to the final. Having won a French Open title, Kafelnikov will be really tough to beat.

I've managed to get right away from tennis today — playing golf at the Capital with dual British Open winner Greg Norman. Greg's always been someone I've respected enormously and to play a round of golf with him is a fantastic experience.

The first thing you notice about Greg is how normal he is despite winning two majors and having been world No. 1 for so long. He is absolutely down to earth and a bloody great player — not that you would know it from his demeanour. He is also incredibly fit and his attitude to everything he does and his preparation for it is first class. It's a real eye-opener to be with him.

The final Saturday brings one of the best experiences I've had at a Grand Slam.

Jonas and I win the doubles title in a huge match. It takes three hours and 16 minutes before we put them away 6–3 4–6 6–4 6–7 (10–12) 6–4 in front of an incredible crowd comprised of Australia's most identifiable band of tennis supporters, the Fanatics, and the Swedes. The Fanatics is a group of tennis enthusiasts led by Warren Livingston, a good knockabout bloke from Sydney.

The fact it was my first appearance in a Grand Slam final in my own country meant the win was huge.

'It's the first time I've been up in front of you guys. I never thought it would be in doubles,' I said in my acceptance speech at the presentation of the trophy.

'I was happier out there than when I won my second US Open.

'To Jonas, we were thinking of going our separate ways after a couple of disappointing performances last year; so thanks for putting up with me.'

It was a thrilling match for everybody and played in great spirits. Mahesh and Leander are incredibly crafty players who are able to play the sort of wristy shots most players wouldn't attempt.

We had a match point against them in the fourth set and then they won the tiebreak 12–10. There were only six breaks of serve in the match. None was more crucial than our break against Paes in the tenth game of the fifth set.

With the score at 4–5 (30–40), Jonas flicked a fantastic return crosscourt, the Indians pushed up a scrambled volley and I was able to hit an overhead for a winner.

On match point, I felt a huge buzz and then a sense of relief and satisfaction.

Some great players have won the Aussie Open doubles and, with a lot of my friends and family in town, there's going to be a huge party tonight. The only low point of the day was being called to do a drugs test, which I regard as a pretty pointless exercise given the Korda furore. It seems if the ITF's independent appeals committee reckons you're a good bloke, you can get away with it.

The frustration quickly passes, however, when the doubles celebrations begin.

A group of about ten people came up to my room for dinner. I feel more comfortable eating in — I'm not so much on display. We ended up venturing out to Heat nightclub at Crown. Little Killer was the first to leave at about 6 am when he had go out and do some coaching. The rest of us hit the sack to recover as the Australian Open drew to a close.

Hingis won the women's singles in straight sets over Mauresmo, clearing the way for Enqvist and Kafelnikov.

As is so often the case, the final was a fizzer. Enqvist started well, but then Kafelnikov got on top and simply wore him down. Thomas seemed to have left his best form in the locker-room.

Kafelnikov is a different kind of character. Very determined and ambitious.

He has now won two major titles and he's a threat on just about every surface. It seems only a matter of time before he gets to No. 1.

As for me, it's time to return to Brisbane to fulfil some commercial obligations.

My next tournament is in Scottsdale, Arizona, at the beginning of March. I'm planning to make the most of the break.

Brisbane and Sydney

CHARITY WORK

The last chapter in the Davis Cup dispute involving Mark Philippoussis and John Newcombe and Tony Roche has finally been written.

After being unavailable for selection last season, in retaliation at Rochey's decision not to travel with him at the end of the 1997 season, Mark is back in Davis Cup tennis again.

The main thing now is that he's back. He's been named in the squad to play Zimbabwe in Harare along with myself, Todd Woodbridge, Mark Woodforde and Lleyton Hewitt.

It's the best news the team could hope for. Now we have to make it work.

Flip is glad to be back, too, admitting he had missed playing for Australia.

'I was very upset about what happened,' he was quoted as saying. 'I love playing for my country and that's what I want to do. I want people to realise that.'

The cynics immediately seized on Mark's renewed availability, claiming there was an ulterior motive — Olympic selection.

Under ITF regulations, players wanting to contest the Sydney Games have to be available for one Davis Cup in either 1999 or 2000.

Newk — having copped a ferocious bagging for what happened with Mark because of his association and friendship with Rochey, the fact that he is Davis Cup captain and also because of the events in Mildura — is unconcerned about peripheral issues, preferring to concentrate on the bonus of having Philippoussis back.

'Mark and I have talked,' he said. 'We're both determined to make this thing work. You don't know what will happen, but I don't anticipate another blow-up.

'I think all of us want to put the last 12 months behind us and put our energy towards the future.'

Apart from resolving the original issue behind Mark's unavailability — Rochey's decision not to travel with him at the end of '97 — Mark and Newk also discussed Pat Cash's outburst at the Australian Open.

'We spoke about that and I haven't got a problem with him,' Newcombe said.

'It is a matter of letting bygones be bygones and also of being very professional about the job we are asked to do for Australia — which is trying to win a Davis Cup match.'

Cash also helped the healing process.

'Mark is keen to play and he wants to win it,' Cash said. 'He wants a bit of revenge and that's the main thing. I think all the guys realise they can win it, so they are pretty fired up.

'I don't know exactly what went on between him and Newcombe and I don't really care. I'm happy he's playing Davis Cup because it's great for his tennis.'

For everybody's sake, I'm hoping the matter is closed. Once and for all.

With Mark back in the team, there's no reason why we can't win the Davis Cup this year.

I had caught up with Mark in Melbourne. We had a couple of chats about playing again and, as far as I'm concerned, the past is irrelevant.

He is very positive about the Davis Cup and that's all that matters. He just needs to start hanging out with the guys again, as he has in the past, and there won't be any problems.

I'm back in Brisbane, having recovered from the doubles victory party, but there's important business to take care of. With the help of my family, I've founded a charity to help homeless children. It's called the Pat Rafter Cherish the Children Foundation.

I'm hoping to encourage the public and large corporations to donate money to the fund. The money will be used to support welfare groups and charities which are working to improve the quality of life for disadvantaged children.

I am very fortunate to have been brought up the way I was in Mount Isa, in Brisbane and up on the farm at Eumundi.

Nine kids makes a big family, but our parents always worked really hard to give us what we needed. They sacrificed a bloody lot for us kids. I remember going to church and watching Dad put money into the various collections.

The charity is an extension of that. I've been fortunate enough to do well financially out of what I love doing and I think I have a responsibility to help those less fortunate in our society. Especially the kids who, through no fault of their own, find themselves out there struggling.

The press conference to launch this charity will be one of the last media commitments I'll make this week. I need to take time to recharge my batteries after the Australian circuit. And there's nowhere better to relax than on Queensland beaches and golf courses, with the added bonus of having my family around.

The week comes to an end all too quickly.

My sister Louise has played a big role in getting me involved with the Youth Off The Streets program in Sydney.

Louise wrote a story explaining the family's attitude towards the project:

Mum and Dad have always told us: 'We trust you.' I remember going to a party a few years ago with some friends from school.

When Dad dropped me off he could see kids wandering in with bottles, so he said to me: 'Just give me a call if you want to come home early.' At the party, a lot of the kids were already drunk or stoned. Someone said: 'There's some stuff over there' — although the ones who had tried it were out of control.

It didn't take long for me to decide there wasn't much happening for me there, so I left at 10.30 pm.

Patrick and I now realise how fortunate we were, growing up in a large family that made us appreciate the simple things in life.

Things like going camping and interacting as a family were important.

Mum would spend almost a year preparing for the annual camping holiday.

You can imagine it — she had one baby in her arms, one in her tummy and six kids running around.

It was this upbringing that made Patrick decide he wanted to give something back from the money he has made from tennis. He gave $350 000 of his winnings from the US Open to the Starlight Foundation to fund a leisure room for terminally ill children at Brisbane Hospital.

But he wanted to do more to help others.

So he asked me to go and see the work of Youth Off The Streets in Sydney. I met kids who had been sexually abused and others on drugs at one of the rehabilitation homes.

When I told him what I had learned, his mouth just dropped. He just said: 'Oh my God. How lucky are we?' I told him it was important that he get involved. It would be good for kids to see that high-profile people were prepared to make a stand against such things and to have a role-model.

His response was: 'Let's kick this drugs issue in the guts.'

Life doesn't have to be complicated; it can be simple. Mum and Dad were always saying to us all: 'Look out for each other' When Patrick is away, I do hospital visits for him. I take his posters along.

I'm not Pat, but I pull my long hair back so I look a bit like him.

The kids say 'You aren't Pat' but when I say 'Sorry, here's a poster', their faces light up.

Patrick had looked forward to discovering first-hand what the kids in central Sydney were experiencing. He played basketball with some of them. He wanted to interact with them.

I think I learned more about the less fortunate on the day of the launch than I had in my whole life.

The day started with a press conference at Star City, where we outlined the aims of the foundation.

Then I met a bunch of street kids, about thirty in all.

They were aged between 11 and 16. Many of them were heroin addicts and most of them had been sexually abused. There were some incredibly sad stories.

Father Chris Riley is doing a fantastic job helping these kids and he needs all the help he can get. It's not an easy job and there's a lot of frustration involved. Father Chris has dedicated his life to the service of others and he's an inspiration to a lot of people. There's no ego involved and not much thanks either, but he's doing incredible work.

Going to Cabramatta that night to play basketball and mingle with some kids in the Youth Off The Streets program was a real eye-opener. There were some amazing stories of hardship and misfortune. The whole exercise served to show me how fortunate I am having the family and friends I have. I don't know if playing basketball with the kids is going to help them, but I am serious about trying to make a difference.

Being on the tennis circuit, where the players are extended lavish hospitality, is sometimes a little distorting.

It can be difficult to put yourself in the shoes of others, but the kids of Cabramatta — and others like them — help to bring you back to earth.

I played basketball with them for about 90 minutes and it was an enlightening experience. You could see how much the kids appreciated me being there, but the sad reality was that as soon as I left they would probably be straight down some alleyway shooting up or whatever.

We really need to make a visible difference for these kids. I want to be able to build a facility for them where they can detox and undergo rehabilitation away from the evils of the street.

Unfortunately, the night ends all too quickly and it's back to business.

AMERICA

Scottsdale to Miami

THE HARD
YARDS

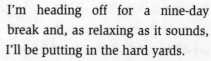

I'm heading off for a nine-day break and, as relaxing as it sounds, I'll be putting in the hard yards.

There's no substitute for hard work and even though it's more than three weeks to the Franklin Templeton Tennis Classic in Scottsdale, I won't be easing up.

After Scottsdale, I'll be going to Indian Wells, then Key Biscayne — which is regarded as the fifth major — and then it's off to Zimbabwe for the Davis Cup.

There's a lot at stake all round, so I want to be in peak condition when the pressure is on.

Andre Agassi has occupied the spotlight this week, earning a default during a second-round match in San Jose against Cecil Mamitt for swearing.

Agassi is occasionally a strange character on court.

I remember playing him during an exhibition in Melbourne and he swore his head off. All of the comments were directed at himself and, given the fact there was no prize money or ranking points at stake, there was no heavy-handed decision-making on the officials' behalf.

But Agassi evidently stepped over the line in San Jose.

It was the second time Agassi has been defaulted in US tournaments, which is a shame considering his high profile in the sport, to say nothing of his influence.

Whatever was the trigger in California, Andre's been around long enough to keep his mouth shut.

If he'd done that, he would probably have won the match.

It turned out to be a great week for Australian tennis. The tournament was eventually won by Mark Philippoussis. Todd Woodbridge and Mark Woodforde won the doubles and no doubt silenced some of the people who believe the Woodies are past it. The Woodies haven't had their most productive year, but they've been clearly the best team in the world since they teamed up in 1991. Jonas and I played them at the Australian Open and managed to win a very tough five-setter.

It's only when you see them close up and in that kind of competition that you really appreciate how great they are. They are still the best doubles team in the world.

Flip is on target for a top-five ranking.

Sometimes you never really know where his mind is, but this time he looks to be on the brink of something special.

If Mark continues to play at this standard, there's no reason why he won't win a Slam. Equally, there's no reason why Australia won't win the Davis Cup.

Before actually getting to enjoy my holiday, I stopped off for a couple of days in Los Angeles.

I was there to do a photoshoot with Ray Ban. There was also a session with *GQ* magazine.

Both shoots involved the photographer getting plenty of shots of me without my shirt. I enjoyed the whole thing, but I sometimes wonder if I'll ever be required to wear a shirt.

An incredible amount of time and effort goes into the shoots, and helps give me a better appreciation of what Lara goes through with modelling.

We were down at Malibu, which was a buzz. I would have preferred to have been chilling out in the water if it were possible, but at the end of the day, this is work.

When we first got to the beach, the weather was very overcast so we ended up at this fantastic mansion. It's supposedly worth $15 million and owned by a gentleman who is a tennis fanatic.

He'd played host to quite a few tennis players over the years, including Newk, Rochey and Ken Rosewall. He was a wonderful host to us as well.

After finishing the Ray Ban shoot, it was time to do *GQ*. This time we ended up at another beachside mansion just down the road.

It turned out to be a long day.

In the evening, a mate and I kick back at the Whiskey Bar in the Sunset Marquee Hotel in West Hollywood.

The Whiskey Bar is incredibly intimate. There's room for only 40 people and this night the pop star Marilyn Manson is there.

It's a really cool place. Tiny, but very popular. The spillover crowd hangs out in the lobby and there's a huge line-up outside the hotel.

It's my favourite bar.

From LA, I'm heading up to Whistler with Lara. Then it's across the States and out to Bermuda and home.

A couple of years ago I had to make a choice about where I wanted to establish an overseas base. The options were London, Monte Carlo, the US mainland or Bermuda. For a lot of reasons, I chose Bermuda. It is laidback and a touch remote, yet still close to the US. Most of the Aussies now have homes in the US, mainly in Florida, but I prefer living out in Bermuda, where a few other players have also chosen to live.

As much as I want to relax in Pembroke, the main urban centre on Bermuda, with the weather, the beaches and the golf courses, I know Rochey and the other boys will be waiting for me in Texas.

And knowing Rochey, he's going to take great delight whipping me into shape if I get to Scottsdale unprepared.

So there's only one thing for it and that means plenty of work — every day.

Scottsdale is one of the fastest-growing areas in the United States. It is one of the suburbs of Phoenix, Arizona. There are a lot of golf courses and resorts here.

The weather in Scottsdale is comparatively mild. It's spring in the desert and so the temperatures are bearable. The locals leave in droves in summer.

Michael Tebbutt lives here. Tebs grew up in Sydney but he went to university at Flagstaff, so he knows the town very well.

We're staying at the Scottsdale Princess Hotel, which is pretty expensive by any standards. The golf course adjacent to the hotel is unbelievable and Tebs, myself, Lleyton Hewitt and his coach Darren Cahill take advantage of the opportunity to test our games on the layout they use for the Phoenix Open.

'Killer' Cahill is a stylish golfer, and Tebs and Lleyton just love competing.

By night, some of the boys go exploring the city. Scottsdale has gallery walks by night, when it's possible to visit more than a hundred different art galleries in the city.

I've drawn Alex O'Brien in the first round. He's a Texan, so he's sure to have plenty of support. He's a pretty competitive character and loves to get stuck into a dogfight.

Thankfully, I manage to get through in straight sets, but there's still plenty of room for improvement.

And just to spice things up, my second-round opponent is none other than Lleyton Hewitt.

It would be nice to pay him back for Sydney. It would be even better to really have my game cranked right up.

Unfortunately for me, Lleyton is too good again and his form — as well as my lack of it — is going to make it really interesting for the Davis Cup selectors.

In fact, with the match against Zimbabwe less than a month away, my selection in singles is far from cut-and-dried. Just because I'm in the squad along with Mark Philippoussis, Mark Woodforde, Todd Woodbridge and Lleyton, doesn't mean I'm going to be selected.

I've got a lot of ground to make up before I can put my hand up to play in Harare. At the moment, it's not happening for me. I need a lot of matches to find form and confidence.

On current form, Lleyton is a real chance to play singles. Lleyton has an amazing ability to lock into an opponent and wear him down with pure competitiveness. He rarely makes a mistake, which is pretty good for a kid who has just turned 18.

And I can see no reason why Jason Stoltenberg shouldn't be involved, even though he lost in the first round at Scottsdale.

Because of the loss, I've decided to play the Atlanta tournament next month. I realise what I need more than anything right now is matches.

My plan was to play fewer events this year, but I gain confidence from winning matches. As such, playing in Atlanta makes a lot of sense and is a logical entree into the claycourt season.

Right now I've got to get across to Indian Wells. From there it's down to the Lipton Championships in Key Biscayne, then the Davis Cup in Zimbabwe, and after that I'm off to Hong Kong for another tournament. Then I'll come back to Bermuda and play doubles at the Bermuda challenger with Paul Kilderry before I fire up for the European claycourt season leading into the French Open.

The last time I played a challenger — a lower-level tournament — was back in 1994, somewhere in Queensland I think. It's simply a matter of getting as much match practice now as I can.

Other than the Bermuda challenger, I'm cutting down on my doubles. I really need to get my head down in singles, and even though it sounds attractive to play doubles in Key Biscayne with Jonas, I mightn't get over to Zimbabwe as soon as I could. I really don't want to be hanging around playing doubles if I lose early on in the singles.

It has been a really crazy season so far. Pete Sampras lost to Jan-Michael Gambill in Scottsdale and he's clearly going through a patchy period.

Gambill, the great American hope to succeed Sampras, reaches the final along with Lleyton.

Lleyton has made a huge effort, considering he had to come through qualifying. It's difficult not to think of Lleyton as a kid, but there he is every week, knocking over guys who have been around for years. He secured a place in his second final of the season by defeating one of his boyhood idols, Mark Woodforde.

But Lleyton can't quite pull it off as Gambill notches up the first singles win of his career. He has already had a great season. Two finals and his ranking is now pushing towards the top 50.

From the thin air of the Arizona desert it is a long drive into the California desert — it is definitely easier to fly in those puddle-jumpers from Phoenix to Palm Springs. Indian Wells is the site of the season's first

Super 9 series tournament on the ATP Tour, which are the top-level events on the ATP Tour and usually feature most of the players in the top ten. Indian Wells is nestled in the magical Coachella Valley. Tall palm trees sway gently across resorts that spare no luxury. Golf courses are designed by only the finest architects and hotels blend perfectly with the surrounding landscape.

Looking down upon the valley are the San Antonio mountains, jagged and rocky, often with traces of snow on them. In the early hours of the day you can see hot air balloons gliding in the distant sky.

The Coachella Valley also takes in Palm Springs and Rancho Mirage and Mission Hills, where Mark Woodforde and Rod Laver live. It is a playground for Hollywood types: the finest cars and the longest stretch limos move along Highway 111 between the valley and Los Angeles.

Indian Wells has a sort of casual sophistication. Roads are named after celebrities — there's Gerald Ford Road, Bob Hope Drive, Gene Autry Trail and Dinah Shore Drive. It's also a place that many retired people migrate to, because of its year-round temperate climate. Goran Ivanisevic once described it as 'God's waiting-room'.

It's against this backdrop that I've drawn German Nicolas Kiefer in the first round. Kiefer is a bit of an Andre Agassi clone. There was a stage in his career when he dressed exactly like Agassi and his game was pretty similar.

He's always had a reputation as the sort of player likely to do very well. He's worked previously with Boris Becker and he's a bloody good returner.

Since my game revolves around the serve, I'm going to have to be at my best.

There's also the added incentive of the world No. 1 ranking.

In fact, there are four players with a chance of succeeding Sampras: Kafelnikov, Carlos Moya, Alex Corretja and myself.

Unfortunately, I won't be getting to No. 1 this week. Kiefer is too solid from the baseline and wins 7–6 (7–2) 3–6 7–5.

In Scottsdale last week, I thought my serve was pretty ordinary. This week it's just plain awful.

Having protected my knee by not practising my serve, I pay the price. I know I've got a lot of work to do on my serve and I really have to pull my finger out.

Hewitt has another win over Mark Woodforde.

As for the world No. 1 battle, there seems to be a bit of a jinx on the contenders.

Kafelnikov is already out, I'm gone and today Mark Philippoussis knocked over Corretja, recovering from a set and a break down. There was a time when Mark would probably have lost that kind of match — and Corretja is no pushover, either.

There was an ominous touch about Flip's win and I've got no doubt he can win the tournament, provided he applies himself with the same tenacity for the rest of the week.

As fate would have it, Flip nailed Moya, the last of the guys in the running for the No. 1 ranking, in the final.

The score — 5–7 6–4 6–4 4–6 6–2 — hints at the scope of Mark's performance against a bloke who has won a French Open and has few peers from the baseline.

It was Mark's first win at a Super 9 tournament, and his second win of the season. Add to that the Hopman Cup success (although most players continue to think of that event as an exhibition) and there's a case to be made for Flip as the most effective player this year.

Pat Cash is certainly impressed by it all.

He believes Flip is the best all-round player on the circuit outside of Sampras, and when you see Flip in full flight it is difficult to argue.

Cashy predicted Philippoussis could win Wimbledon if he was able to reproduce his Indian Wells form. It was a big call, but who could argue after what he'd done in the California desert? By a quirk of the rankings computer, Moya ends up being No. 1 after reaching the final.

Following Indian Wells is another of the big events on the ATP Tour, the Lipton at Key Biscayne, which is part of the Miami Keys.

These keys (cays or low islands) are a bit of a distance from the Florida Keys and the more famous islands of Key Largo and Key West.

Key Biscayne is reached by the tollway on the Rickenbacker Causeway from the downtown area of Miami. The road cuts across waterways — on one side you have Miami Bay and on the other is the ocean. The colours of the water are quite incredible. The hues of pale blue blend into a deeper blue and gradually change into the most magnificent aquas. More often than not the water is like a sheet of glass broken only by the white froth churned up by jet skis skimming across it.

Miami promotes itself as the 'Cruise Capital of the World' and when you see all the liners you can understand why. Yachts are moored at the marina, which is attached to the restaurant called 'Sundays' and cruise liners slip slowly out to sea with holiday-makers.

The tennis facility is one of the nicer ones on the Tour. It took the Buchholz brothers many years and even more in legal battles to get their way in building it. Only during the two weeks of the event, which has undergone a name change to the Ericsson Open, are the stands allowed to be higher than the palm trees.

The rest of the year you would never know there was a tennis facility there if you looked at it from a distance. It is quite amazing how the vegetation on Key Biscayne has regenerated, because the island was in the direct and incredibly destructive path of Cyclone Andrew a few years ago.

For the first time in months, Sampras finds his name at the bottom of the draw as the second seed. Moya, as the new world No. 1 — only the 16th in history — is at the top.

Sampras, doubtlessly stung a little by the demotion, says he doesn't care.

'If it was a priority, I would have gone down to Australia,' he said.

'It doesn't matter what you're ranked in February or March. December is the important time. It's always been an end-of-the-year-goal for me.'

Sampras is also at pains to point out that he is not in decline.

'I'm not going to be done with this game anytime soon,' he said.

'Travelling for ten years, 30 weeks a year, gets a little tiring, but I still love competing.

'These next four or five years, I'm going to give myself an off-season of two or three months just to chill out, like the guys do in other sports.

'That will hopefully help me have a long career.'

As ever, the Aussies are out in force.

And, just for something completely different, Lleyton Hewitt and Mark Woodforde are drawn to play against each other. Lleyton wins again — 6–2 6–1 — to earn a crack at Mark Philippoussis.

Scotty Draper beat the Argentine Mariano Puerta and Andrew Ilie got through against Galo Blanco, of Spain, to be my second-round opponent.

As one of 32 seeds in Key Biscayne, I got a first-round bye.

Knowing the way Andrew plays, I'm going to have to stay focused. He's extremely energetic and hits the ball with enormous power.

If he gets on a roll, as he did at the Australian Open in January, he can be awfully tough to stop.

Thankfully luck goes my way and I've made it through to the third round and waiting there for me is Kiefer.

Having lost to him in Indian Wells, I made the comment that I wanted to 'serve it right up to him'. My comments are predictably seized upon and the match is promoted as a grudge match. However, I don't know of any player who likes to lose, let alone two matches in a row to the same player.

Kiefer just happens to be someone I want to beat. With my form at the moment, I'd be happy with a win — any win.

Kiefer is not in an obliging mood, however, and he beats me 7–6 (7–5) 6–4.

With the way the match was hyped, it's hardly surprising that there's a fair bit of post-match interest in my thoughts on Kiefer.

The simple truth is that Kiefer was too good for me. He's become a more consistent player and he's a lot stronger mentally. He used to be fragile if you could get on top early.

I told the media I was quite impressed with the German.

Kiefer, by all accounts, was on pretty good terms with himself.

When asked about the supposed feud between us, Kiefer grinned and said, 'It's normal that he's not happy because he lost to me. I beat him a second time. It's perfect. For him it's not so good.'

As they say, winners can do what they like.

It wasn't a great day for Australia. Mark Philippoussis was beaten by Russian Marat Safin in straight sets. Flip had earlier knocked out Lleyton Hewitt, so at least I knew I would have a practice partner if I left early for Harare and the Davis Cup tie.

It would have been tough for Flip to back up his win in Indian Wells at the Lipton Championships, which is a significant event in its own right.

'A loss is a loss,' Philippoussis said after the match. 'I'm very disappointed, but now I'm going to train hard and get ready for the Davis Cup.'

Flip intends to go back to his home in Longboat Key, which is on the west coast of Florida, to prepare for the Davis Cup. I'm heading up to New York, then across to Johannesburg and up to Harare.

Before I head off, though, we take one last opportunity to go out and enjoy the Florida nightlife. We have a great night, which is made more memorable — for all the wrong reasons — for the fact Kilderry nearly lives up to his name and kills us all by accidentally driving through a red light.

Little Killer was the designated driver and as sober as a judge, but he just lost concentration for an instant. It could have been a disaster.

Harare

DAVIS CUP

From that near-miss it's over to
Harare, via New York and
Johannesburg and, as one of the
guys with the team said on arriving
at Harare's colonial-style airport,
'It's payback time.' Rochey, Muddy
Waters and Andre Bizas, the team
physiotherapist, are already in Harare, along
with Fenton Coull from Tennis Australia. We're
staying right in the middle of town at a five-star hotel. The
luxury of the hotel contrasts vividly with the poverty and hardship of life
on the street.

For all its natural riches, Zimbabwe is still an underdeveloped country.

We're told not to venture out on the street on foot at night, but we
discover some great restaurants out in the suburbs.

The Zimbabweans clearly fancy their chances, and who could blame them after the win in Mildura last year? The Black brothers, Byron and Wayne, are idols in Harare, which is understandable considering what they've achieved, not only on the ATP Tour, but also in the Davis Cup, both at home and abroad. They might not have been the most prolific winners on the ATP Tour, but Byron has won a handful of singles titles and both he and Wayne have won a lot of doubles events.

We head down to the City Sports Centre in the morning for our first training session and you could say it was a bit of a shock. When Lleyton and I arrived for our first hit there was no net in place. The workmen found a piece of string, which we stretched from the net posts and used as a temporary barrier.

The court itself was fine. It was hardcourt and had been laid over a cement base, which is usually employed for basketball matches.

The stadium is also used for boxing matches and hockey. The design of the place is quite different. It is a bit like a barn and before the International Tennis Federation officials arrive to put up the advertising, the wind whistles in through the doors.

In the circumstances it would have easy to have been distracted. The workmen hired by the Zimbabwean Tennis Federation gradually spruced the place up. The acoustics are quite amazing. The sound of the ball resounding off the racquet reverberates around the stadium and it is overwhelming to think how much noise the passionate local crowd will produce.

Working on the practice court with Lleyton is great for my game. My serve is the one area that has been concerning me for a while. The knee soreness I suffered at the end of last season has been a constant concern since I ruled out having an operation.

But this is a huge tie for Australia and it's no time to be hedging bets.

Rochey finally lets up on us and we head back to the team hotel, initially along a pot-holed bitumen road before we get to the main highway.

The sights and sounds of Africa are as close as the car window.

Everywhere you look, you're reminded of the vastness of the continent.

There are a lot of different markets on the sides of the roads, some for food; there are others in the city centre for stone carvings and assorted pieces of art.

There is a lot of poverty in and around the city. The homeless live in makeshift shelters within metres of five-star accommodation. Attempting to reconcile the cruelty of life can be disheartening at times.

Even though we are outnumbered in terms of support, we are not completely without backing.

Rod Marsh has a squad from the Australian Institute of Sport's cricket academy in Zimbabwe for a series of one-day matches and he intends to have some of his squad come out to the tennis. We're hoping to go down to the Royal Zimbabwe Sports Club after the tie to have a look at a match. The AIS has helped develop a string of Test cricketers for Australia under Rod's direction.

We'll also have the support of Warren Livingston — an apt name on the African continent — in his role as head of the Fanatics, who travel to our overseas ties from all parts of the world.

We're eating in most nights. There's a very pleasant French restaurant at the hotel.

We visit the Australian ambassador's residence with the rest of the Australian contingent and it turns out to be a nice evening.

It's great to be surrounded by Australian voices in a foreign land. Rod Marsh is also there, along with Tennis Australia officials and a few of the media.

The Zimbabweans are desperate to prove the win in Mildura was not a fluke and we are very quickly put on notice that this is not going to be a cakewalk.

Newk makes a speech about the mystique of the Davis Cup. He and Rochey were at the 1953 Davis Cup at White City, both watching as kids on a day when the famous old Sydney venue was filled to the brim with a record crowd that's never been surpassed. Newk reckons he was imbued with the Davis Cup spirit that day watching the Australians and the Americans go head to head.

There is something about the allure of the Davis Cup that transcends normal tournament play and it's a shame that some players don't embrace it the way they should.

For some players, the Davis Cup is the sole opportunity to show their nation how much they care about representing their country.

Goran Ivanisevic said being the flagbearer for Croatia at the 1992 Olympic Games was the highlight of his career. Boris Becker also carried the flag for Germany.

The US players have always had a diffident attitude towards the Davis Cup. There have been some notable exceptions, of course, and few have set a better example than Jim Courier.

The Davis Cup is the one thing I would love to win before I retire. It would mean so much to have that achievement after what we've been through as a team, losing to Hungary in 1995 and having to claw our way back into the world group.

But that's a lot easier said than done and Zimbabwe is not going to lie down for us. Byron and Wayne Black are really good blokes who have busted themselves to do their best for Zimbabwe every time they play.

They've done an amazing job, especially when you consider it is basically one family representing a country. For them to beat an established tennis nation like Australia away from home was huge.

Now they want to do it again.

With Lleyton as my training partner, I'm quickly under the pump. Lleyton is just about the perfect training partner for me because of his fantastic returns. The Black brothers are not big guys and they're not going to blow you away with their groundstrokes. But they can chop you up with their returns and they're a damned good doubles team because of that.

I've been fortunate enough to play doubles with Byron. In fact, I did so in Hong Kong after we lost to Zimbabwe in Australia last year. As much as we hated losing then, the only satisfaction — if that's what you can call it — was the fact it was 'the Black Stump' and Wayne, who's known as 'Stumpy', who were the ones to do it.

Wayne is yet to arrive in Harare after winning the Lipton doubles title with Sandon Stolle, but tonight we're off to dinner at Byron's place.

His house is simply jaw-dropping and has an incredible view. It is cut into the side of a hill and looks down a valley. There is a swimming pool out the front in a fantastic natural setting.

If ever you wanted evidence of what hard work can bring, Byron's house is it.

The Black brothers have been the most successful players in the history of Zimbabwean tennis and are a tremendous example of what can be achieved from limited opportunities.

All of the guys really enjoyed the evening at Byron's house. The fact we're able to sit down over dinner with the so-called 'enemy' so close to competition-time says much of the spirit between the two teams.

Back on court, Lleyton Hewitt's practice form is drawing plenty of attention and for all the right reasons. I believe he deserves his chance to play and have said as much. My form is still a way off, but I can slowly feel it returning.

Whether I can regain it before the tie starts remains to be seen.

Flip rolls into town with his good mate Charlie Tsadaris and immediately goes to work. It is the final step in reuniting the team.

There is no tension and Newk and Rochey are clearly at ease with Mark back in the fold.

Newk is at pains to play down the issue with the media.

'I can't foresee any problem,' he said. 'It would be silly to say everything is the same as what it was because a lot of things have been said and done over the past 12 months. But this is the Davis Cup and Davis Cup means representing your country. You are not representing yourself.

'We have all got a job to do here and that is to give 100 per cent on and off the court so that Australia can try and win a Davis Cup match. That overrides everything else.

'If there are any personal animosities, I would think as we are professionals, they should be put aside.'

Newk is obviously keen to lay to rest any old issues, without making any bold statements about the future.

'I hear a lot of things,' he said. 'But in all my conversations with Mark there hasn't been an angry word spoken. I certainly don't have an axe to grind and I don't see any problems sitting next to Mark. I've always been a big fan of Mark's tennis and I'm no different in that regard to what I was five years ago.'

Newk's main concern is my serve. He had one of the great serves and it doesn't take long for him or Rochey to spot any small technical glitches.

We've been working on the serve for the past couple of days and there are now some very good signs. And when my confidence in my serve returns, my whole game benefits. If there is a bit of zip off the surface, it gives me the chance to get right into court and make a good first volley. It's basically the difference between having to volley off my toes or have a comfortable waist-high volley.

Newk thinks I'm ready to improve by 10 per cent, which would be nice considering my record on the circuit going into the tie is seven wins from 13 matches.

Flip, by contrast, has won 17 of his 20 matches — which is the best record in the world at this stage of the season — and he's shown little sign of having trouble adjusting to the 1500m altitude. We practise twice today, once in the morning and then for an hour after six to get used to the lighting when darkness sets in outside.

Mark consents to an interview with the small Australian media pack — News Limited, Fairfax and Channel Seven — and it is immediately obvious he wants to put the past behind him.

'Everyone is very professional here,' he said. 'We know we have to come together as a team and we're doing that. I'm definitely a lot more mature. I'm just growing up in every way and it's showing in my life and my tennis. We'll all be very relaxed here. Newk will be making a few jokes on the sidelines. All I want to do is to compete to my fullest. That's what I've been doing and that's why I'm where I am at the moment.'

Flip's presence is a boost for us in every way. He's won every match he's played in singles against the Black brothers and we're naturally hoping he continues.

There has been a little time in between training to enjoy the sights and sounds of Africa.

Lleyton and I take up the opportunity of getting out on the golf course. There are some beautiful courses here, but nothing compares with the wildlife.

We organise a tour of a game reserve on the outskirts of Harare and although there is a high fence around the perimeter of the park, it is easy to think you're out in the middle of the African wilderness when you venture deep into the park. We saw the big five — lion, elephant, rhinoceros, water buffalo and leopard — and really enjoyed being so close to some magnificent animals.

It is when you meet these creatures in their own environment that you realise how powerful, strong and well-adapted they are. I would recommend the experience to anybody.

The selectors have settled on the team and Flip and I will play the singles, with the Woodies to contest the doubles. The Black brothers will play in all the matches for Zimbabwe.

The official draw is conducted among heavy security at the home of Zimbabwean president Robert Mugabe.

There are armed troops and police everywhere. We are taken in by car and escorted from the carpark to the venue of the draw, which is an open-sided marquee on the lawns in front of the President's residence.

It is searingly hot and all the players wish they could dispense with blazer and tie, but we're unable to. Zimbabwe's First Lady, Mrs Grace Mugabe, presides over the draw after making a short speech about the virtues of competing well and with dignity. Against this backdrop of apparent serenity and goodwill, there are undercover security officers everywhere.

Eventually Mark Philippoussis is drawn to play the opening match against Byron; I play Wayne in the second match. The doubles, as usual, will be played on the Saturday and Zimbabwean captain Gavin Siney has resisted the temptation to promote former South African Kevin Ullyett into the doubles team. Actually I think it was Byron's decision. He virtually runs the team.

I'm scheduled to face Byron in the first match on Sunday with Flip to play Wayne in the second of the reverse singles.

We pose for photographs with Mrs Mugabe in front of her home, which is colonial in style and features a massive stuffed lion on the porch.

After the mandatory post-draw interviews, it's back to the hotel to prepare for a light hit and an evening of massage and relaxation.

No matter how many Davis Cup ties you play, there is no way of avoiding pre-match nerves. In fact, you'd be worried if they weren't there. This tie is no different. I'm bloody anxious, given what happened last year and the fact all of Australia will be watching.

Flip is also understandably nervous. He's got a 3–0 record against Byron and, leading by two sets to one, he seems certain to post win number 4.

Unfortunately, it is not to be. The noise in the stadium is almost sufficient to burst an eardrum as the small contingent of Australian supporters is drowned out by the raucous Zimbabweans.

Flip serves 45 aces, the highest in his career, but loses 6–3 3–6 4–6 6–3 7–5 to Byron in a cliffhanger. I didn't see all of it, but I certainly heard it as I tried to prepare in the change-rooms, not really knowing what was going on out on court.

The crowd was chanting the ancient Shona hunting cry *yave hyawa yokugocha* which roughly translates to 'the meat is on the barbecue' or 'that guy, he's as good as dead meat'.

The pressure is now really on as I go out to play Wayne Black. There is nothing like the Davis Cup to fire the passions and after winning the first set 6–3, I manage to lose the second with an ordinary service game.

Midway through the third-set tiebreak, the fate of the tie is really in the balance but I scramble through to win 7–4 and then take the fourth set 6–2.

Once I got on top of Wayne, I really wanted to nail him psychologically.

I ran to a lead of 5–0 before he got a late break and then I closed it out.

Winning aside, the best thing was the way I served. It was imperative that we didn't begin to trail 0–2. Now at least we're back where we started and hopefully the Black brothers are feeling the pinch a bit ahead of the doubles.

The Woodies are really pumped for this match. Like all of us, they were victims of circumstance in Mildura last year. Todd was ill with the same virus I had and was ruled out of singles contention despite being a Wimbledon semi-finalist on grass. And Mark was told early in the week before the tie to concentrate on doubles and not to worry about singles.

Unfortunately for Pecker, he was then summoned in as an eleventh-hour replacement for me when I couldn't recover after losing to Byron on the opening day. Worse still, Mark was then beaten by Wayne Black and it is history now how Byron came out and beat Stolts in the deciding fifth rubber.

So the Woodies have much to play for and it showed immediately.

They won a tight first set 6–4, but quickly lost the second as the crowd became involved in the match. It was then that they really turned it on and suddenly the barracking, dancing and shouting became a little less obvious.

The boys really got on a roll and careered away to win the last two sets 6–3 6–0 to put us 2–1 up with the reverse singles to play — but it's far from over.

I've got to play Byron in the first match and basically the whole tie now hangs on it.

The score was ultimately 6–4 7–6 (7–2) 6–2 in my favour, but it was a lot tighter than that. Blacky had four break points in the first set and I was lucky to play my best match in a long time when it really mattered. I think fatigue might have been a factor with Byron. He had played a five-setter against Philippoussis, then sat through his brother's singles match before losing a demoralising four-setter to Mark and Todd.

And after losing the second-set tiebreak to me, I think he became a little disheartened and wilted a touch after I broke his serve in the opening game of the third set. That was the breakthrough I needed and I was very pleased to be able to finish the match off. Having secured the tie 3–1, the boys were obviously very happy, but we still had some unfinished business.

Flip duly took care of it, increasing the margin of our win to 4–1, which carried us into a quarter-final meeting with the US in Boston — which is another matter altogether.

The Davis Cup works on a home-and-away rotational system and we played the US in Washington in 1997, so this year's quarter-final ordinarily would have been played in Australia. But because of a decision taken three years ago by the ITF, we have to go back to the States and play the Americans in Boston.

The reason for all of this is the Davis Cup centenary.

The first match was played 100 years ago between the US and Great Britain.

Australia did not have a team in the competition then, so there are a couple of issues in dispute here.

Centenaries and anniversaries are meaningless to me. I'm the type of person who lives from day to day. I don't think too much about what a certain day means, especially in a historical sense.

And that's why I've objected to the US being given successive home ties.

If the ITF really wanted to mark the celebrations in an appropriate fashion, they could have played the first-round tie of this year's competition between the US and Britain. They had the perfect opportunity. But because the weather wasn't suitable for an outdoor tie at the Longwood Cricket Club in Boston, they decided not to switch the match indoors from England to the States.

As a result, Australia has had to forfeit the home-ground advantage and the boys are pretty annoyed about it.

We discussed the issue over the victory dinner in Harare and the following morning Newk and Geoff Pollard, the Tennis Australia president, sent in a protest to the ITF.

The Americans, typically, are sticking to their guns.

But we've based the appeal on three grounds — Melbourne Park's 15 000 capacity is three times that of Longwood Cricket Club's; Tennis Australia is as at least the equal of the US Tennis Association in its capacity to stage anniversary celebrations; and, when all is said and done, it's our turn to host the Americans.

The ITF has attempted to sweeten the deal by offering to play successive home ties in Australia, but that's a vexed issue, too.

Who's to say when Australia will have a team like the current one again? We've got a world champion doubles team in the Woodies, a Grand Slam finalist in Mark Philippoussis, one of the rising stars in Lleyton Hewitt, and myself and the other guys, including Jason Stoltenberg, Andrew Ilie, Sandon Stolle and Scotty Draper.

And it could be ten years before the US is drawn to play us again.

That's why the players were barracking hard for Greg Rusedski to beat Jim Courier in the fifth rubber of the Americans' tie with the Poms.

Jim is a fantastic bloke and most of the time I love to see him doing well. But we'd have loved to have played the English at Melbourne Park on clay for the right to go into the semi-finals.

Unfortunately politics — and the Cup centenary — have got in the way.

The team has had a great night. It feels as though we are a unit again and we're all determined to accomplish our goal of trying to win the Cup for Australia for the first time since 1986. We believe we have the team to do it.

Hong Kong and Bermuda

THE WAR OF WORDS

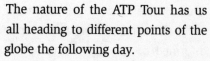

The nature of the ATP Tour has us all heading to different points of the globe the following day.

Lleyton Hewitt heads back to Adelaide on the same flight as Newk and Rochey and a few of the boys. Flip is going back to the States and I'm off to Hong Kong for a tournament.

Lara will meet me there so I've got a lot to look forward to.

The tournament is played at Victoria Park, which sits on the island but is nestled far enough away from the noise and pollution of Hong Kong to be bearable. I have fond memories of the stadium. It was here in 1995 that I won an exhibition for a lot of money and I'm keen to show the form that I produced against the Black brothers in Zimbabwe.

I've got the German Bernd Karbacher in the first round and he's a tricky player. I won the first set in a tiebreak, lost the second set the same way and then fell away badly in the third set to lose 6–7 (4–7) 7–6 (7–1) 6–2.

I was very disappointed, mostly because it was a pretty ordinary effort on my part. I was mentally tired, but that was no excuse. The conditions were different to those in Zimbabwe and, for some reason, I found it extremely difficult to see the ball — which is a problem I rarely encounter.

If I was annoyed at losing to Karbacher in Hong Kong, it was nothing compared to my anger when I found out the Americans are now pushing for the quarter-final tie to be played on clay. How much do they want?! They have got a home tie out of turn, they have reneged on a discussion involving John Newcombe at the US Open last year when the US Tennis Association indicated the match would be played on a neutral surface and now they want to play on claycourt, a move designed to disadvantage our team and help Jim Courier's cause.

Newk has been on the telephone to all of the players, keeping us informed of the latest developments. The short story is that we're not happy and the spectre of a boycott has arisen.

We can't believe how arrogant the USTA has become over this issue. It claims that since the US is the host nation it has the right to the choice of surface. That, however, is contrary to what we understand.

It has got to the point now where the guys couldn't care less about the Davis Cup centenary, nor the apparently divine right the Americans think they have to hold the tie in Boston. Australia is being penalised already by not playing on home turf; why should we concede any more ground? If the USTA continues to push us too far, and ignores the ITF's directive to play on hardcourt, I'm prepared to boycott the tie if that's what Newk and Rochey want.

Mark Woodforde and Todd Woodforde are really ticked off about it, too. There's a part in all of us which says 'stuff them, we won't play' and there's another part which says 'let's go over there to Boston and kick their backsides'.

This whole issue has been wearing — basically a distraction we can all do without.

The Americans are sticking to their guns, despite being ordered by the ITF to abandon plans to play the tie on claycourt.

The issue has been picked up by the international press and the boys are fielding questions all over the world.

Mark Philippoussis, for instance, was asked about it in Monte Carlo and, like the rest of us, was emphatic the match should be played in Australia and, if not, then the Americans should not be allowed to lay clay.

'We deserve to play the matches at home,' Philippoussis said. 'Playing at home is so positive for the players. We can draw 14 000 people in Melbourne, and they are only talking about 5000 in Boston.

'If they want a historic event, why didn't they switch the first round match against Britain? All the other Australian players feel the same way.'

Eventually the war of words is settled with a meeting between Geoff Pollard, the USTA's Judy Levering and Brian Tobin of the ITF.

In effect, the Americans are forbidden to put down clay. In return, Tennis Australia has to guarantee the next two ties between the countries — which will both be played in Australia — will be played on hardcourt.

Call it a moral victory if you want, but the point stands that we should not be heading to Boston for the match in the first place.

I head back to Bermuda to play a challenger event for the first time in years with Kilderry.

'Little Killer' is so-known because Darren Cahill is the original — and he would say the best — 'Killer'.

Kilderry is a great mate. He is good company socially and he's pretty handy on court, too, having been a Wimbledon junior semi-finalist. I'm using the break to get home to Pembroke and prepare for the claycourt season.

I've arranged to play a singles exhibition for a mate of mine from Bermuda as well as taking part in the doubles with Little Killer. I can't remember the last time I played at that level, probably back in Queensland in about 1992.

I'm sure it's going to be a lot of fun. The rest of the time is taken up with practising, a bit of golf and fishing. The waters around Bermuda are fantastic.

As much as I want to relax, though, I've got to keep my eye on what's ahead — which is the slow, red clay of Europe and lots of long rallies with, hopefully, the sun on my back.

It's actually a pretty nerve-racking experience playing at home in Bermuda in front of a lot of friends.

Kilderry and I should have lost in the first round of doubles, but we scraped through.

Courtside announcer Hughie Barrett took every opportunity to stir up Kilderry. As we walked on court for each match, his voice would boom out: 'Ladies and gentleman, this team has achieved earnings of $8 million, but only $5000 of that is Kilderry's.' Hughie's humour took some of the nerves away. It was very comfortable being able to compete at a tournament just down the road from my home.

We managed to play a lot of golf and we got out to Mid Ocean, my favourite course, quite a bit and had the odd Dark and Stormy, a Bermudan concoction of Gosling's rum and ginger beer.

We mostly ate out, but there were times when Killer persuaded me to cook a few vegetarian garden burgers on the grill.

As usual we rented mopeds to get around the island. The speed limit for cars is 30 miles per hour (about 60 kmh) and it's quicker and easier to get around by moped. Killer spends most of the time picking himself up from the grass.

While I was home I did a couple of magazine interviews. One was for *GQ*, the other was for *Vogue*. Kilderry, in his own inimitable way, contributed with a couple of incriminating comments about some of our locker-room antics.

The challenger is every bit as enjoyable as I imagined it would be. We actually turned up on court one day in Bermuda suits and shorts.

Unfortunately for Little Killer, it seems the Australian Open doubles champion is more of an impediment than an inspiration and we lose the final to Richey Reneberg and Doug Flach. But the tournament has served its purpose as I get ready to head off to the ATP Challenge in Georgia.

Atlanta

ATP CHALLENGE

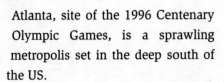

Atlanta, site of the 1996 Centenary Olympic Games, is a sprawling metropolis set in the deep south of the US.

It is renowned as the home of Coca-Cola, CNN (the Cable News Network, owned by Ted Turner, husband of Jane Fonda) and some of the biggest freeways in the world.

Unfortunately on this day, the freeway — or beltway, as it is known here — is mayhem. There's been an accident and I've been stuck in traffic with literally nowhere to go. I had telephoned Kilderry to ask him to warm up with me two hours ago, but 50 minutes later I'm still sitting in the hotel carpark.

There's not a thing either the driver or I can do. It is simply a matter of waiting.

So much for arriving early to prepare for my match with Martin Rodriguez of Argentina.

I've scouted around for information on Rodriguez. He's been around for a long time and he's had some decent wins, but he was beaten in the last round of qualifying. He's been given a second chance to reach the main draw after an injury to another player, so he's got nothing to lose.

I know I'll have to be on my game.

But I didn't play very well at all and lost to the 101st-ranked player in the world.

It's disappointing to lose early, any place, any time. It doesn't matter what the circumstances are. The simple facts are that I need matches and I need to be winning them. At the moment I'm not.

But I'm not the only top-ten player to be struggling at the moment. Pete Sampras, Yevgeny Kafelnikov and Goran Ivanisevic are also going through some tough times and it is the performance — or lack of it — of the top players that has pushed appearance money into the spotlight.

Appearance money has always been a controversial issue in tennis. Some players take their guarantees or appearance money no matter how they have played or the degree of effort they have put into their matches. There is no doubt that some players 'tank' (deliberately lose) sets.

I've seen it happen a lot and there have been some really obvious tanks.

A controversy blew up at the Czech Open in Prague this week when the tournament directors refused to pay Ivanisevic and Kafelnikov $150 000 each in guarantees.

I wasn't there and I didn't see them play, so I can't comment on whether they tanked or not.

I've seen Kafelnikov tank sets, but I haven't seen him tank a match. I would be surprised if he did that.

He's obviously going through a tough period at the moment, adjusting to life as world No. 1 after winning the Australian Open in January. Maybe he's taking his troubles onto the court with him and that's always a dangerous thing to do.

With Goran, you never quite know what's going through his mind. He can have some big wins and some bad losses.

If players have performed badly, it's the tournament director's prerogative to withhold the guarantee.

The Petr Korda issue just won't die. It seems as though the Australian Open happened a long time ago, but I'm still asked questions about Korda.

It's strange to be in the same change-room with a guy who would be out of every other sport in the world for testing positive to a steroid.

What's more surprising is that nobody has sledged him, which is probably more a reflection of tennis as a sport. I haven't heard of anybody having a go at him and nobody really gives it to him upfront, but there is definitely a feeling around the place about him.

People are finding it hard to look him in the eye because he's been found guilty of taking something he shouldn't have and he hasn't been made to sit out of the game like he should have.

The whole thing has become a joke and a lot of players are still annoyed about it.

Rome
ITALIAN OPEN

Dusseldorf
WORLD TEAM CUP

Paris
FRENCH OPEN

Halle and Rosmalen
EUROPEAN GRASS

London
WIMBLEDON

EUROPE

Rome

ITALIAN OPEN

I'm in Rome for the start of the Italian Open and the beginning of my campaign on European clay. After Rome, I'll go to Hamburg for the World Team Cup — an invitational event to the eight nations with the best combined rankings of its two leading singles players — and then it's down to the French Open in Paris.

My form this season hasn't been what I would like, but I feel great after the work I've done this week with Muddy Waters in Bermuda.

Knowing you've done the hard work really helps you mentally. I'll go into these next three tournaments with the attitude that whatever happens, happens.

It releases a lot of pressure that way and I can go out and play a free-flowing game without worrying about what might happen.

If I do that, and the conditions are hot and dry in Paris and the ball can move around for me, I know that my best form is just around the corner. I'm not concerned about when my form returns. That doesn't really matter. The only thing that matters is that it's on the way back.

Little do I know how quickly the form will return.

I'm staying at the Hilton Cavalieri on a hill overlooking Rome, the Eternal City, where the pasta is out of this world and the people are impossibly chic.

The Italian Open is a Super 9 and there are some attractive ranking points at stake.

The tournament is played at the Foro Italico, which was built by the dictator Benito Mussolini as part of the glorification of Italian sport during the country's fascist regime.

The Olympic swimming venue, dating from 1960, sits next door and the River Tiber is not far off in the distance.

The architecture is amazing and the atmosphere is almost gladiatorial.

The players walk down a long corridor before breaking into the bright sunlight — shades of Christians being thrown to the lions — to reach centre court.

The centre court is constructed of marble and surrounding the arena are these fantastic statues from Roman times. The bleacher seating is constructed around the statues, which seem to peer through the narrow spaces between the lines of spectators like ancient sentinels.

In short, this is one of the great arenas in the world. And it is hot.

I've got Goran in the first round. He's one of the really good blokes on the Tour, but his form has been very erratic this season.

I know if I can stay with him he'll give me a chance.

Sure enough, after a tight first set, Goran fell away quite badly, losing 7–5 6–0.

It's a good win for me and it's amazing what a little bit of confidence can do.

There's nothing like a win. You can feel good in practice, but it's far removed from being in a match situation and coming out in front of world-class guys. Goran is exactly that. He's been No. 2 in the world and has reached three Wimbledon finals.

Next up is a talented young Argentine by the name of Gaston Gaudio and after what happened against Rodriguez in Atlanta, I won't be taking any chances. I need more wins to boost my confidence and I'm left satisfied with a 6–2 6–3 victory.

I religiously avoid looking any further into the draw than my next match and I have good reason to stick with the habit since Andre Agassi awaits in the third round. There's a lot of talk now among the European media.

Sampras has lost to Fernando Meligeni and there's a lot of speculation over his future.

Pete's struggling this year and there's even suggestions he might be past his best. He was whistled off court by the Romans and he later described his form as disgusting.

The doubts have arisen because of Pete's injuries and inconsistent form this year. It's true — Sampras hasn't had a good start to the year, but he's still a great player.

There's no question he's definitely in a slump and, at this stage, he hasn't shown the form of previous years. He's been troubled with a back problem this year and he's lost early again this week in Rome.

But as the winner of 11 Grand Slam titles, Pete is not somebody you can afford to muck around with. I've been fortunate enough to have beaten him in the last two matches, but there are plenty of other guys I'd rather play.

You still have to be very careful around him and you just know that he's going to come back at some stage.

Before Sampras is counted out, people should remember what a great champion he is. And who knows what goals Pete has set himself this year? Holding the world No. 1 ranking for a seventh consecutive year, winning another major to equal Roy Emerson's record and possibly a sixth Wimbledon title are likely to figure high in his thinking.

The match against Agassi pans out perfectly and there's plenty to play for. If I win the Italian Open, I go to No. 1.

But first I've got to get past Nicolas Lapentti. An Ecuadorian, Nicolas has played a lot of claycourt tennis and he's had a really good year, reaching the semi-finals of the Australian Open.

I know it's going to be tough. He's pretty fit, like most claycourters, and he's prepared to stay out there all day.

But I'm confident about my fitness, too, even though Lapentti wins the first set 6–4 and the second set gets really tight. I squeeze it out 7–5 and breeze through the third 6–1. Just as I'm getting my breath back, I learn that next up I'm playing Felix Mantilla, who's a great baseliner. He comes from Spain, which basically equates to a long, hard day at the office.

Before I go out on court Alex Corretja jokingly tells me he's going to let me win the final if we both get there. It's a big ask. I have to take care of Felix; Alex has Gustavo Kuerten, who's playing really well at the moment.

I fulfil my part of the deal by winning 6–3 7–5 against Felix. The balls are lighter in Rome this year and, with the way the weather is, I can get into the net behind my serve and the footing is typically shifty, so some of the baseliners are having trouble getting set to play their shots and then moving off in the same motion.

The conditions are pretty similar to what I encountered in Paris two years ago for the French Open when I got to the semi-finals basically by mixing things up with a bit of serve-volleying and baseline rallies.

Kuerten is going to be awfully tough. He's a French Open winner and he's already won Monte Carlo this season. The way he's playing right now, very few people in the world can go with him and I'm expecting a really tough match. Still, I've done plenty of work and the ball is coming off the racquet nicely. All the work Muddy and Rochey have pumped into me is paying off.

'Guga', as Kuerten is known, is in no mood to roll over simply so I can say I'm No. 1.

The first set is tight and goes his way 6–4. I start to build a bit of momentum in the second set and there are some chances to go to break points, but I just can't get there and it was really important that I win that second set. It is a best-of-five-sets final and to trail by two sets to love in the heat against a player such as Guga is not a good scenario.

Kuerten basically didn't give me a chance and he deserved to win. I would have loved to have had my name on the trophy, and it would have been nice to have got to No. 1, but it wasn't to be.

There's a reason for everything and, in the end, it was a really tough ask against Guga.

He has now won Monte Carlo and Rome, two of the biggest events outside the Slams, and I think on clay right now he's the best player in the world.

His results have shown that.

He's timed his run into the French Open perfectly. He's got enough tennis under his belt and he's spent this week surfing down in Biarritz.

I nearly got back into the match against him in Rome, but I really needed to win the second set.

I had some momentum going in the second set and then I played a pretty ordinary game to drop serve. In the third set I had more opportunities to go up a set point, but I didn't take them.

I tried not to think too much about the ranking until I got to the final. I guess we'll never know how generous Alex was prepared to be.

The Italian Open is an important event and Alex is one of the world's best claycourters.

Dusseldorf

WORLD TEAM CUP

From Rome it's on to Dusseldorf and the World Team Cup — I believe its correct title is the World Team Championship and, in a way, it's the ATP Tour's version of the Davis Cup; the difference here is that you get invited to the tournament on the strength of your world ranking. The tournament director Horst Klosterkemper is one of the nicest people you could hope to meet. Because I was in the final in Rome he organised a private jet to get us to Dusseldorf in time.

This is really a phenomenal tournament, held at a private tennis club, the Rochusclub, in a very upmarket part of the city. The tournament is packed out every day and it is quite incredible how all the spectators fit in. Sometimes it can be an effort getting from the practice courts

TOP: LINING UP A BACKHAND RETURN AT THE LIPTON CHAMPIONSHIPS, KEY BISCAYNE.

BOTTOM: TAKING A BREAK COURTSIDE.

Top: Out for revenge. The playing Australian Davis Cup team in Harare. Left to right: Mark Philippoussis, me, Mark Woodforde, Todd Woodbridge and captain John Newcombe.

Bottom: Mucking about with Lleyton Hewitt.

DESPITE THE OFF-COURT HOSPITALITY OF THE BLACK BROTHERS, I WAS IN A RUTHLESS MOOD ON COURT.

TOP: THE SUPPORT OF WARREN LIVINGSTON AND THE FANATICS
WAS A REAL INSPIRATION IN HARARE.

BOTTOM: THE BOYS ARE BACK IN TOWN!

RIGHT: OFF TO A GOOD START AT THE ITALIAN OPEN. GUSTAVO KUERTEN SHUT ME OUT IN THE FINAL, DENYING ME THE WORLD NO. 1 RANKING ... AT LEAST FOR THE TIME BEING.

BOTTOM: STADE ROLAND GARROS, PARIS. MY STAY AT THE FRENCH OPEN LASTED ONLY THREE ROUNDS.

SOMEHOW I MANAGED TO PULL OFF THIS RETURN BETWEEN MY LEGS!

CLIVE BRUNSKILL/ALLSPORT

Top: Taking
stock of the
situation.

Bottom: Attacking
the net is an
integral part
of my game.

Practising at the Heineken Trophy, Rosmalen.

to the locker-rooms and clubhouse but the security people get us through.

There are about nine claycourts for the eight teams. Two of them are match courts and the schedule has teams taking it in turns to feature on centre court one or centre court two. For 51 weeks of the year the suburb where we play, or more particularly the street where the club is situated, is in a quiet, leafy part of Dusseldorf. The back of the club has a beautiful forest and the trees are still so fresh with the spring leaves — they are a bright green.

It's a very nice setting. The fans who come out to watch are passionate in their support for all the eight teams — we are split into two groups and play round robin with the top two teams going into the final — but obviously when the German team comes out, they barrack loudest. The clubhouse itself is not very big but nothing at the event is a problem for anyone. We are looked after very well, with each team having a hostess to take care of our needs.

Australia draws Slovakia first up. We scrape through, even though I lose my match against Karol Kucera. Mark Philippoussis gets us out of a hole to level at 1–1 and then Sandon Stolle and I get us home in the doubles.

It was a real confidence-booster.

Next we play France and the quality of players is impressive. I've got Cedric Pioline next, and he's a mercurial character. He's capable of beating anybody on a good day and then he can go out and lose in really hollow fashion.

He's been a US Open finalist and also a finalist at Wimbledon. He's also been in the semi-finals of the French Open, so he's got a very good record without ever probably doing justice to his talents.

Memories of the huge match I had with him in the Davis Cup in Sydney are never far away and I think they're in the back of Cedric's mind, too, as we settle down for a tight first set. I got the feeling that if I could get on top of Cedric early, then there was a good chance he might fall away a bit in the second set. That was exactly what happened as I eased to a 7–6 6–1 win.

Flip and Sandon continue to impress. Mark has such a big game that he's a threat on all surfaces and Sandon is a vastly underrated player.

He's played in the Davis Cup and has won a US Open doubles title. He's such a talented serve-volleyer it's a pity he hasn't been able to cement a place in the top 100, but he always keeps pushing through. He's had the added pressure of being the son of a great player — French and US champion Fred Stolle, who works as a commentator with Newk on Channel Nine at all the overseas majors — yet he is still very down to earth.

Having built a 2–0 record, we've played ourselves into a pretty good position. If we beat the Americans tomorrow we go straight into the final. Andre Agassi has pulled out with a back problem which, on the surface, does not bode well for his campaign for the French Open, but the US still has Sampras — a formidable-enough obstacle in anybody's language.

I haven't played Pete since the US Open last year when a fair bit was made of his injury in the semi-final. In fact, there was a lot said about our match at Indianapolis, where I was given the match on a second-serve ace. Pete thought the call was wrong and made his point abundantly clear to just about everybody who cared to listen.

I was annoyed at the time that he went on about it for so long. I would have loved to have put him away without any excuses at the Open, but it wasn't to be. So there's a lot riding on our match tomorrow and it would certainly be a great match to win.

Pete is clearly uncomfortable on the clay and I gradually get away to win 6–3 7–5. It's another nice edge to have over him, even though he's not playing at his best. We wrap up the contest 2–0 when Flip wins his singles and then Pat Cash partners Sandon in the doubles.

The result of the match was irrelevant, but it was obvious the competitive fires still burn within Cashy.

He has been desperate to play all week and had taken the liberty of putting his name down on the team sheet.

As captain of the Australian team — it's a pretty loose arrangement based on ranking — I'd told Cash that if the opportunity presented itself and if either Mark or I needed a rest, he could play.

Unfortunately for him, he couldn't quite get a win.

Sweden, winner of the last two Davis Cup titles, awaits in the final.

The Swedes love nothing more than the team format and, in much the same way Australia unites for the Davis Cup, Jonas Bjorkman and Thomas Enqvist are hellbent on providing Sweden with another victory.

And for much of the day that's how it threatened to pan out. Jonas beat Flip and I was down a set and a break to Enqvist, who was playing on probably his second-best, if not best, surface.

I needed to win the match to keep the tie alive into the doubles. I could feel that I wasn't that far away even after Thomas won the first set. When he's on, his first serve and forehand are among the biggest in the game. But if he's slightly off, he can be vulnerable.

I was able to pull back into the match gradually after losing the first set 7–5 before winning the last two 6–3 6–3. There was a short interval before the start of the doubles and Sandon was pretty fired up, like the rest of us, to cap off the week with the win.

Australia hadn't won this event since 1979 and this was clearly our best chance.

But we still had some pretty formidable opposition. Whenever Jonas stands across the net from you in doubles, you have a match on your hands.

Fortunately, we played a really smart match, everything fell our way and we ended up with the championship. Having not yet experienced the joys of Davis Cup triumph, this felt pretty good and served only to whet my appetite for a win in the Davis Cup.

But with the French Open looming large, the Davis Cup will have to wait a little longer.

As we leave Dusseldorf for the short trip south-west to Paris, the full extent of a dispute between Boris Becker and Nicolas Kiefer becomes apparent.

Becker is the Davis Cup manager and is generally revered in Germany where his feat of winning six Grand Slam titles and becoming No. 1 in the world, helping win the Davis Cup and basically being the German tennis flag-bearer makes him virtually untouchable.

His role in semi-retirement has been to plan for the future and to ensure there is no end to the production line that has provided talents such as Becker, Steffi Graf, Michael Stich and Anke Huber.

Part of his deal is to run the elite Mercedes Benz squad, which is a finishing school for the outstanding young prospects. Kiefer, until recently, had been part of the program, but there was a fallout over the Davis Cup when Kiefer allegedly refused to play because he wasn't feeling well. Becker was apparently furious with Kiefer and made his feelings known.

There was more trouble in Dusseldorf as the Germans plummeted out of contention and it now transpires there was another argument between the pair. Becker is not happy, neither is Kiefer.

As Australia has come to understand over the past couple of years, disputes like these can ruin team harmony and sabotage overall goals such as winning the Davis Cup or the World Team Cup.

Winning the World Team Cup in Dusseldorf last week was one of the most satisfying achievements in my career.

As the name suggests, it is a team event and everybody — from myself and Mark Philippoussis to Sandon Stolle and Pat Cash, who stepped in to play doubles — pulled their weight.

Only the top tennis nations get a guernsey at the event and it's on clay, so for Australia to win in the circumstances was quite an achievement.

The Davis Cup has always been a huge thing for me and there's an obvious parallel between the Davis Cup and the World Team Cup. My form in the Italian Open flowed over onto the slower courts in Dusseldorf. I was stoked with the win against Thomas Enqvist, coming back from down a set.

He'd cleaned me up at the Australian Open so I was glad to get a win over Thomas. To follow up in the doubles with Sandon was the icing on the cake.

Paris

FRENCH OPEN

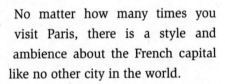

No matter how many times you visit Paris, there is a style and ambience about the French capital like no other city in the world.

As usual, the traffic is incredible. The *peripherique*, the multi-laned highway which circles Paris, carries an enormous amount of traffic and today is no exception.

We're headed for the Warwick Hotel, where I always like to stay for the French Open.

Paris is a city to be enjoyed by day and night, but my overwhelming focus for the next fortnight is the slow, red clay of Roland Garros.

As tournament sites go, this is about as good as it gets.

Everything is done with incredible style and attention to detail. This is one venue in the world where the player feels as though he is the focus of attention, not in an egotistical way, but simply because every comfort is lavished on us. From the car service to the food to the locker-room facilities, the French Open has it all.

Stade Roland Garros is named after a French pilot who was killed in the First World War. As memorials go, it is superb.

It sits on the fringes of the Bois de Bologne, a huge mass of greenery and parks which effectively serves as the lungs of Paris. You can walk for ages through the parks next to Roland Garros.

This complex is the home of the French Tennis Federation and history oozes out of the place. The centre court is one of the most atmospheric in the world with its white-grey stands and ivy-clad walls. The crowd seems close and loud.

The players' enclosure is perfect. It's right behind the court and there are few better viewing platforms in any sport.

One of the most famous courts actually sits next to centre court. It is now third on the pecking order behind centre court — or *court centrale*, as the French call it — and court Suzanne Lenglen, the swish new show court named after the greatest French player of all time, but court one is fantastic.

It is separated from centre court by the Musketeers' Square, where statues of the four most famous male French players stand. The musketeers are Rene Lacoste, Jean Borotra, Henri Cochet and Jacques Brugnon — who brought enormous success to tennis in France in the twenties and thirties and are now part of French tennis folklore.

Court one is circular and around the top of the grandstands are inscribed the names of the champions. On court, it is very much like a coliseum. When you're in there the crowd is right on top of you and the atmosphere is amazing.

Close your eyes for a second and it's not impossible to imagine the greats of the past doing battle on the same court.

It's been 30 years since an Australian has won the French Open but I'm hoping to smash the hoodoo at Roland Garros over the next fortnight.

Such a thought would have been a joke a couple of weeks ago, but my results at the Italian Open and my form in Dusseldorf at the World Team Cup have given me a lot of confidence going into the French.

Now that I'm hitting the ball well again, what I really need to cap things off is hot dry weather in Paris.

That's how it was two years ago and I surprised myself — and a lot of others — by making the semi-finals.

I played basically the same sort of tennis in Rome, where it was really hot and the ball really moved around a lot for me and I was able to play serve-volley tennis on clay. Hopefully I can do the same thing in Paris. Obviously that's going to be tough.

There have been a lot of very good serve-volleyers, including John McEnroe and Stefan Edberg, who have reached the final of the French Open only to fall at the final hurdle.

If the weather is hot, then I think my chances improve.

Being seeded third means there's a bit of an advantage for me, but the really crucial thing is the draw. If I can get through the early rounds relatively easily, then I can work my way into the tournament.

What you don't need — particularly at the French — is a couple of five-setters early on. If you get caught in a couple of long matches, then you can really pay the price later on. If you survive.

I'm feeling really positive about my game at the moment, which is a great sign.

There's not a whole lot of difference in the way I'm playing now from early in the season, but my confidence is definitely up.

To beat Agassi, Ivanisevic, Lapentti and Mantilla on clay has done a lot for me. Hopefully it can continue in Paris.

I think the Aussies are in for a big tournament.

We've got Mark Philippoussis, Lleyton Hewitt and Jason Stoltenberg going well. And there's blokes like Richard Fromberg, Andrew Ilie and the Woodies, who always lift for the Slams.

Frommy had a win over Yevgeny Kafelnikov in Prague recently and everybody knows how tough Frommy can be on clay.

The women's side is looking positive, too. Jelena Dokic has got a wild card into the main draw, which is fantastic, and Alicia Molik and Nicole Pratt are also straight in.

There's a good feeling about the whole tournament. Hopefully one of us can break the drought. I'd love to be the one to do it.

As ever, the first couple of days are crammed with upsets. Mark Philippoussis couldn't continue his good form out of Dusseldorf and lost to Jason Stoltenberg.

I think the fact Mark was playing another Aussie was pretty important.

Stolts had the game to stick with Flip, who served for each of the three sets.

I got through 5–7 6–3 6–0 6–2 against Swiss 18-year-old Roger Federer, who had a great season in the juniors last year when he won junior Wimbledon and finished the year ranked No. 1 in the world in juniors.

I made a rusty start against Federer in the first round and paid the penalty by dropping the first set.

But I got myself back into the groove and won comfortably in the end.

Federer's going to be a good player. He's got the game and the attitude to get to the top. And he's also coached by Peter Carter, a former professional who comes from the Barossa Valley in South Australia.

I was a little frustrated in the first set but I gradually got into the match and the confidence I had from winning the World Team Cup clicked in and made all the difference.

To have Australia break through after 20 years in Dusseldorf — and especially in the heavy, slow conditions — has really set us up well for the rest of the year.

There's not too much opportunity to stop and smell the roses, as the Americans are wont to say, because Nicolas Escude is my second-round opponent. He's an Australian Open semi-finalist and has the capacity, like many of the Frenchmen, to hit a lot of winners very quickly.

Predictably, this turns out to be a testing clash for a number of reasons.

There's nothing more frustrating than getting on top of your opponent only to have the match stopped because of rain.

And that's exactly what happened as I led Escude 7–5 6–0. In that situation you just have to stay positive, remind yourself how well you're playing and come back and finish the job.

I was pretty annoyed when I lost the third set 6–2 when play resumed, but I was able to win 6–4 in the fourth.

I'm also in the doubles with Jonas, but with the rain delays the schedule of matches has started to build. In fact, I'm feeling pretty tired and I'm beginning to think the idea of playing singles and doubles at the majors might not be what I need after all.

But there's a lot to play for over the next eight days or so. With Yevgeny Kafelnikov, Pete Sampras and Richard Krajicek out of the way, talk has already started about the No. 1 position.

My goal is to win the tournament and to do the best I possibly can.

If I manage that, the ranking will take care of itself. There are just too many things that can happen in between for me to be looking any further ahead than my next match.

If I could control one thing, though, it would be to ensure the weather stays hot and fine.

As involved as it sounds, a few degrees of warmth can really make a significant difference to the pace of a claycourt. When it's hot, it's more like a hardcourt, which I love.

I've obviously got a lot of reasons to hope the rain has made its last appearance.

The weather duly clears, but I can find no solution to Fernando Meligeni's determination and steadiness from the baseline.

I really hit the wall and after dropping the first two sets 6–4 6–2 I came back to win the third 6–3. Unfortunately that was the end of the line for me as Meligeni deservedly won the match 6–3 in the fourth.

To tell the truth, I felt buggered.

But, in the way that the tennis circuit is structured, there's little time to rest and recuperate.

With my schedule and the way the Tour is set up, I often spend long periods away from Lara.

With her career in modelling and television-presenting, it's not that often that our paths cross.

We're both busy people.

So it was great that Lara has been sent to Europe on a modelling assignment.

The job was for a hair commercial in Greece, which was very convenient considering the fact I was playing events in Italy, Germany and France.

Lara has now been able to join me in Paris and we'll spend some time together.

It's healthy to have supportive people around you, regardless of what you're doing, and Lara and my brother Peter are precisely that at, and away from, the tennis.

The nature of the Tour is such, though, that I tend to travel mostly on my own.

Lara and I travel together when our schedules permit, but when I'm at tournaments I guess I notice the difference to most of the other players.

Many of the guys — and some of the girls, too — travel with a lot of people. It's fine to have a network of friends and coaches, but it's also a personal thing.

I don't travel with a coach. I'm in the fortunate position of being able to tap into Tony Roche at various tournaments. Rochey, in my opinion, is the best coach in the world.

Outside of catching up with Rochey, I tend to limit my travelling partners to Lara and my family. Occasionally, I'll tour with a mate, such as Paul Kilderry or Matthew MacMahon, but I think there is less expectation from others if you're on your own.

That way you can create your own goals and lock in to them.

The French Open locker-room has to be among one of the best in the world.

Virtually everything you could want is on hand, from a massage to a haircut to the typically fantastic French food.

What I do notice the most, however, is the enormous cross-section of cultures. There are so many different countries playing tennis now that it's almost like a gathering of the United Nations at times.

Australia, the US and some of the larger European countries used to dominate the game — and the locker-room — but not any more.

It's interesting to watch the leading players and how they interact with the other blokes.

Rivalry is a pretty strong deterrent from allowing yourself to get too close to certain blokes, but I get along well with the Dutch, Spanish and Swedes.

They're great blokes.

The Aussies, as usual, stick together. I can't think of anybody among them I wouldn't want to have a beer with, from the Woodies and Mark Philippoussis to Kilderry, Josh Eagle and Andrew Florent.

No matter where you are, you always know when there's an Aussie within earshot.

As I prepare to head off to Germany, it's interesting to reflect on the French Open, which has again thrown up its share of mystery players.

If somebody had predicted before the tournament that Fernando Meligeni, Dominik Hrbaty and Andrei Medvedev would be in the semi-finals vying for glory with Andre Agassi, they would have been laughed at.

But they're there and all of them have a great chance.

Meligeni knocked me out in the third round and anybody who can nail Alex Corretja in straight sets on clay can obviously play. A Brazilian, Meligeni is a typical claycourter — lean, runs all day and gives nothing away.

Hrbaty is a Slovakian and has great stamina. He should have beaten Pete Sampras at the Australian Open three years ago when he led 4–2 in the fifth, before Sampras got over the top of him in fierce heat.

He's got a great temperament and he'll build on doing so well at Roland Garros. He's a very capable player.

Medvedev has always been an enigma. He went into the French Open ranked 100th in the world, yet he came out and knocked over Sampras and then thumped the favourite for the title, Gustavo Kuerten.

On that form alone, Medvedev is capable of beating anyone in the world.

He's an incredibly gifted player. He's been as high as No. 4 in the world, but has always lacked consistency for a variety of reasons.

And Andre is Andre. You just never know with him. He was in real strife against Carlos Moya, the defending champion, but he pulled out a fantastic win. He's done well at the French Open before without ever winning it.

On rankings and experience, he was the clear favourite going into the semi-final round.

I was happy with the way I played in Paris, but I think I paid the price for doing well at the Italian Open (as a finalist) and the World Team Cup (as a winner) in Dusseldorf and playing so many matches.

In the end, I felt a bit tired and couldn't stay with Meligeni when I really needed to.

I had the opportunity of going to No. 1 if I'd got to the quarter-finals and I'm disappointed that I haven't achieved that, but it's not something I'm obsessed with.

As I've said, if it happens, it happens. Rankings are the end result of playing well. If I continue to play well, the ranking will take care of itself.

Regardless of what else happens to Andre Agassi at the French Open, his comeback has been one of the most extraordinary in tennis.

His ranking blew out to 140 and he had to go back to the satellite circuit to rebuild his confidence, form and fitness.

That's pretty tough for anybody, let alone someone who's already won three majors and has been ranked No. 1 in the world.

I think Andre realised in Paris that he was very close to achieving history in that if he won the French he'd be the first player since Rod Laver to have won all four majors.

Not even Sampras, John McEnroe, Boris Becker and Stefan Edberg have managed to do that.

The other remarkable thing about Agassi is that he's back playing at a high level after first getting to No. 3 back in 1987. That's a long time in anyone's language.

The other spin-off of Agassi doing well is that his effort will help to revive the sport in the US, where the game has been floundering a bit.

Agassi and Medvedev won their way through to the final, but only after one of the truly great women's finals.

Steffi Graf came back from a set and a break against Martina Hingis, who felt the pressure of the situation and behaved in a way she probably regretted.

Steffi's a phenomenal player and a superior athlete. She never knows when she's beaten and she showed her fitness against Hingis in the third set when it really mattered.

It was her 21st Grand Slam singles title. That's amazing.

The men's final was just as dramatic.

Medvedev won the first two sets and seemed to have the match by the scruff of the neck and then Andre began working his way back into it.

Yet Medvedev never really dropped away. Andre simply kept building and building. He kept the pressure up and refused to go away and got his just desserts.

I don't think anybody in the locker-room begrudged him the success because of what he has gone through with his divorce. It would have been nice for Medvedev to have won as well. He's a bloody good player and a great bloke.

I'm sure his day will come.

The other highlight of the weekend was watching Rod Laver present the trophy to Andre. Laver is a hero to all of the Aussies and we're all delighted he's been able to recover from the stroke he had in LA last year.

Halle and Rosmalen

EUROPEAN GRASS

I'm off to Halle in Germany for the first grasscourt event of the year.

The courts aren't as good as Queen's Club in London but they'll be good for my game because my serve tends to dig into the court and fizz a bit, giving me time to get into the net behind a high-kicking serve.

I'm not playing Queen's for a number of reasons. Their courts are probably too good. In fact, they're more like a slippery hardcourt and it's difficult to keep your footing.

Additionally, I was disappointed with the tournament organisers over an interview I did last year. I gave the interview on the condition the article would not appear in Australia — but it eventually found its way there. I felt Lara and I had been betrayed and you have to stand on your principles or people are going to walk all over you.

So I'll be going to Germany this year and then up to Rosmalen in Holland to try and defend the title from last season.

From there, it's across to Wimbledon for the Big One and I can hardly wait for that, either. The courts at Halle are prepared exactly the same way as Wimbledon, but they're not quite as good. The courtside advertising hoardings also bear no comparison to Wimbledon. But the tournament is obviously modelled on the best tournament in the world, so it should be enjoyable.

I've taken a bit of a punt on the weather being better in Germany than England and that will hopefully mean more practice time.

I'm confident with the way I'm playing and moving at the moment.

It's difficult to absorb everything written and said about you sometimes, but I was heartened to hear John Newcombe predict I could win Wimbledon this year.

As a three-time Wimbledon champion and world No. 1, Newk obviously knows plenty about the sport and I desperately hope he's right.

I'd love nothing better than to be there on the final Sunday at Wimbledon, playing in the singles final.

Having won the US Open twice, winning Wimbledon, the Australian Open and the Davis Cup for Australia remain my highest priorities.

First things first and that means Halle.

Halle is a small town in north-west Germany where the Gerry Weber Open is held. I've come up from Paris, still shaking the red brick dust out of my clothes, with my brother Peter.

It's a relatively unusual site for an ATP Tour event, but I had always heard good reports about it.

The tournament is owned and run by Gerry Weber, a wealthy German clothing manufacturer. It's hard not to be impressed with what they've done with the tournament. From the moment you arrive, it becomes clear no expense has been spared.

The tournament has hired a couple of guys who used to work at Wimbledon and the whole place bears a striking resemblance to the All-England Club.

The courtside advertising signage has the same green tone that Wimbledon uses and the groundstaff have cut the courts in the same way as they do at Wimbledon. In short, it is a dress rehearsal for the Big One.

Away from the courts, the hospitality is fabulous.

When people go out of their way to make a big effort to make you feel comfortable and welcome, you like to repay that enthusiasm with a good performance.

There's a lot riding on this week. If I have a really good tournament, I can get to No. 1 in the world.

I'm up against fellow Aussie Andrew Ilie in the first round and, given the fact Andrew is renowned for his performances on claycourts and hardcourts, it's a pretty reasonable draw.

But you just never know with Ilie. He hits the ball with tremendous power and he's capable of doing a lot of damage if you give him the chance.

I felt pretty comfortable once the match got going and I won the first set 6–3.

The second set was much tighter and I squeezed through it 7–5.

Andrew has still got to get the hang of grasscourt tennis. He's got all the weapons and it's only a matter of time. He smacks his groundstrokes incredibly hard and usually from really unusual places. He certainly is a rare talent.

The word from the ATP Tour is that I basically have to match whatever Yevgeny Kafelnikov and Pete Sampras do over at Queen's Club in London this week if I want to take over from Kafelnikov as No. 1.

Kafelnikov soon ruled himself out of the race when he lost his first match in England. He's been in a slump since winning the Australian Open. I guess some of the hunger has gone from his game.

I can relate to that. Kafelnikov plays a lot of tournaments and, most of the time, in singles and doubles. It is an exhausting combination.

Sampras continues to struggle after another disappointment in the French Open, where he lost to Medvedev, but he's still in contention as I prepare to play Dutchman Jan Siemerink at Halle.

Siemerink wins the first set 6–4 and it becomes pretty obvious this is going to be a tough match. I clamber back to win the second set 6–3 and, mindful of what is at stake, try and finish it off in the third set.

Siemerink won't go away and soon enough we're in a third-set tiebreak.

It goes on and on, and even though I have five match points on his serve, I can't put him away. He wins the tiebreak 19–17. It was bloody frustrating. A win there could have put me in a perfect position. My mood is hardly helped later when I heard that Todd Woodbridge was up a break of serve in the third set against Sampras before losing.

I was obviously not destined to go to No. 1 this week but there's still a chance for me if another Aussie, Wayne Arthurs, can knock over Sampras in the next round. Arthurs has an incredibly powerful left-handed serve and he's a pretty good volleyer, too. While there's life, there's hope.

The match is shown live on television in Halle and a couple of the boys are sitting around watching it. Sampras wins and, when the new rankings come out for the Wimbledon fortnight, Sampras will be back at No. 1 and I'll be at No. 2.

Life is too short to sit around moping about what might have been, so Peter and I, Carlos Moya and Andrew Florent head out to let off a bit of steam. It turns out to be a great night. There are times when you've got to get out and kick back. If you were locked into tennis the whole time, you would probably lose your mind. Europe is one place I can relax without having to worry too much about being asked for autographs all the time.

Peter, Florey and Carlos are good company and we wind it up reasonably late.

I definitely needed the outing.

Losing to Jan Siemerink really hurt.

Not only was the No. 1 ranking at stake — and definitely within reach — but I had set myself for a big tournament.

Going into the Gerry Weber Open, I knew this week was my pathway to No. 1 because of the way the rankings work.

But it was really up to me.

In the circumstances, there's a lot of pain in this defeat — and will be for quite a while.

I felt nervous going into the match, knowing what was riding on it, but I played well.

Unfortunately, I didn't play quite well enough. I can't say I blew it, but I did have five match points, although none of them was on my serve. There were a couple of points, though, I didn't finish off well enough and history says I lost the match.

Siemerink is a great grasscourter. He's a left-hander and got to the quarter-finals at Wimbledon last year. But, all things being equal, I think it was a match I should have won.

Grass requires a funny style. Being solid is sometimes not enough. You have got to take your chances — and there might only be a couple — or you lose. The nature of the surface means you've got to go for winners when you can.

As disappointing as it was to watch the world No. 1 ranking slip back into Sampras's hands, Halle has been a great week.

We've been lucky with the weather and I've been able to get in a lot of practice, which I'm hoping will work in my favour when Wimbledon rolls around.

The tournament has managed to develop two very good indoor grasscourts, which we were able to use regardless of the weather.

Having won Rosmalen last year, I won't be able to make any ground next week in the rankings as I try to defend the title.

But my chance will come again at Wimbledon.

Sampras has got a title to defend and I've never been past the fourth round there. So if I can do well, and the luck goes my way, there could be a lot to celebrate in a fortnight's time.

As much I as try not to think about it, Wimbledon now looms larger than ever, with only eight days to go.

I've never had much success there, so I expect my performance to improve.

No matter what the draw throws up this week, it will be tough. There is no such thing as an easy draw.

There's a stack of great grasscourters, guys like Pete, Andre, Richard Krajicek, Todd Martin, Goran Ivanisevic, Tim Henman, Greg Rusedski and Mark Philippoussis. Any of them could win it.

If I can keep improving and have a little bit of luck, I like my chances too.

Rarely has so much revolved around a Wimbledon championships. There's not only the title at stake over the next week, but also the world No. 1 ranking.

I would like to be No. 1, no doubt about it, but my preference is to win Wimbledon. Of course if I do that, I will become No. 1.

But I can't get ahead of myself, especially since there are ten guys in the running for it.

I have to make at least the fourth round — which I've never bettered here — to have any hope of taking over from Sampras.

Every player has different ways of dealing with the pressure of trying to get to world No. 1.

You're always going to go on the court with a thought that 'if I win this next match I could be No. 1 or I will be No. 1'. You've got to face the fact that it is going to be there and you've got to deal with it the best way you can.

I've cut out all the unnecessary distractions this week and have committed myself to doing only the things I have to do. My sole interest is doing the best I can at this tournament.

When I travelled to Rosmalen last year it was with a lot of disappointment and depression over my form at Queen's Club.

I'm a little flat this time because of the Siemerink match, but there's nothing like the challenge of trying to defend a title successfully to focus your mind.

My preparation is unusual, to say the least. When Andrew Florent arrives, he has nowhere to sleep and ends up sharing my room.

His snoring was shocking.

Despite all that, I'm ready to play Dutchman Paul Haarhuis in the first round. He's more renowned for his doubles exploits these days, but he's had some good singles wins over the years and he's suited to grass.

As it turns out, it was a match I could easily have lost. Haarhuis won the first set and the second went to a tiebreak before I won 4–6 7–6 6–3.

Martin Damm is next. We played the final last year, so he's clearly no pushover. The match went smoothly, though, and I got through 6–3 6–4 before beating Kenneth Carlsen, who's a pretty dangerous left-hander with great reach at the net, 6–3 6–4.

Tommy Haas is my semi-final opponent and I felt myself go up a cog in winning 6–2 7–5 to reach the final where I'll play Andrei Pavel — if the rain ever stops.

As it turns out, the match to decide the Heineken Trophy almost didn't happen.

The final was due to start at 1 pm but because of heavy rain, Pavel and I couldn't get onto the court until 6 pm. The match was about to be abandoned when the tournament staff rang through to the weather bureau and were told the weather would improve.

I'd spent the afternoon trying to keep my mind on the job ahead while monitoring the World Cup cricket final at Lord's in London — so, in a way, the weather was meant to be.

Peter and I sat in the players' lounge watching the final, ball by ball, on the Internet. As you can imagine, there is only limited interest in cricket in the Netherlands, but it was fantastic following the progress of Steve Waugh's team.

If I'd been in London, I would have tried to get a ticket to the final but as it turned out, I had the best of both worlds.

When Andrei and I finally got on court it took me a while to get going and I was lucky not to lose the match in the second set tiebreak.

Pavel is a damned good grasscourter and he had me down a match point.

I got through and won the third set — then I had barely enough time to make the acceptance speech and get down to Rotterdam to catch a helicopter across to London.

One of the things that really impressed me about Rosmalen was the way the crowd sat around for so long in the hope of getting to see the final. Hopefully Andrei and I gave them a bit of entertainment.

Most importantly, the confidence has come back after the setbacks in Paris and Halle. Wimbledon starts tomorrow and I can't wait.

There's no time to celebrate my first tournament win of the year, but it felt awesome.

London

WIMBLEDON

Wimbledon. The very mention of the name conjures images of grass, the sport's greatest champions and tradition. It is the tournament every player in the world wants to win. There is not a player in the game who didn't grow up dreaming of one day lifting the trophy on Wimbledon's centre court.

Most of the greats have won at Wimbledon. There is a handful of players, including Ken Rosewall and Ivan Lendl, who won everything else, but couldn't nail Wimbledon. Having won at Grand Slam level, Wimbledon is the one tournament I want to win above all others.

Hopefully this will be the year.

Lara and I are staying in a house in nearby Wimbledon village. Most of the players rent a property to avoid travelling in heavy traffic into central London.

And if it rains, as it often does during Wimbledon, it is much more convenient being able to stay out at Wimbledon.

I'll never forget walking into the All-England Club for the first time.

You can feel the history oozing out of the ivy-covered buildings, which are ringed by the most fantastic grasscourts you're ever likely to see.

The locker-room also has a lot of atmosphere.

The Aussies always take over a particular corner of the locker-room. The old blokes, mostly Newk, Rochey, Owen Davidson and Ken Rosewall, who happen to be some of the greatest champions the sport has seen, make sure nobody invades our corner.

It is an Aussie enclave and a place noted for a lot of laughs with an occasional touch of seriousness.

Because of the lateness of my arrival in London, I make my first appearance at the All-England Club on the opening Monday and the place is already humming.

The practice complex attached to Wimbledon is Aorangi Park. It's there that I head first to make the transition from European grass to the English variety.

I've got to play Italian qualifier Cristiano Caratti tomorrow.

It's a good draw but I have to make the most of it. As it turns out, everything goes as smoothly as expected after I have adjusted to the Wimbledon courts, which are unbelievably lush and true.

The score is 6–3 6–2 6–2, which sounds impressive, but I know I have to improve dramatically because I'm playing my second-round match against my doubles partner and good mate Jonas Bjorkman.

The Australians make a tremendous start to the tournament and, in a departure from the norm, it is the women who have caused all of the shocks.

Jelena Dokic, the 16-year-old baseliner from Sydney, has thrashed world No. 1 Martina Hingis 6–2 6–0.

All of the boys not involved in matches were sitting in the locker-room watching. It was amazing to watch Jelena go about her game with virtually no nerves at all. Everything she did turned to gold and Martina was absolutely outplayed.

It's been a long time since a qualifier, ranked 129th in the world, has played so well at the Grand Slams. Dokic has been a star in the making for a long time.

She showed at the Hopman Cup in January that she would be a force to be reckoned with and she's gone on with it here.

She played a flawless match. The hard part now will be for her to reproduce that form.

Mark Woodforde, Mark Philippoussis, Andrew Ilie, Todd Woodbridge, Richard Fromberg, Wayne Arthurs, Sandon Stolle and Lleyton Hewitt all reach the second round.

Scotty Draper was beaten by Pete Sampras in the first round in the defending champion's opening match on centre court. Jason Stoltenberg followed later the same afternoon at the hands of Greg Rusedski.

My major concern was how to handle Jonas. But first we've got doubles against South Africans Marius Barnand and Brian Haygarth and it turns into a marathon. I had thought about quitting doubles after what happened at the French Open, but I'd given a commitment to Jonas and, as far as I was concerned, that was the end of the matter.

A five-set doubles match in the first week of Wimbledon is something I don't need and I will sit down and talk with Jonas about it when the time is right.

Obviously with a singles match against him tomorrow, the time is not right now.

It was difficult having to play him a day after we teamed up for a five-set win, but we both respect each other a lot and we don't get right into each other's faces on the court.

We are good mates and we do understand that we can lose to each other on any given day. So you're not mad when you come off if you have lost because you know you may win tomorrow.

There's no aggro out there, so that's a nice way to play.

Luckily in this case, I thought I played pretty well to have a four-set win — 6–2 7–6 (7–3) 6–7 (7–9) 6–2.

Some people were suggesting I should buy Alan Mills, the tournament referee, a beer for making us play on after the third set, when I thought the light wasn't good enough to continue.

Mills wanted us to play four more games and I couldn't see the point of playing just four games if we were going to stop.

But when Jonas and I did start playing again, I was lucky enough to get the breaks and I closed out the match.

Jonas wasn't helped by a leg injury, but I was pretty pleased to have got out of that match with a win.

The really weird thing about the first few days at Wimbledon this year was the fact the weather was perfect in the first week, yet play was being stopped late at night on the show courts because of the 2 pm start, the traditional starting time of matches on centre court and court one, the main show courts.

Tradition is a wonderful thing but, from a player's perspective, there is nothing worse than being frustrated by fading light at the end of a cloudless, rain-free day.

My next opponent is very familiar — Thomas Enqvist. He fixed me up at the Australian Open and I managed to get him back in the World Team Cup.

Grass suits me a lot more than it does Thomas, but he's such a good player, I won't be taking him for granted.

The match works out beautifully. Thankfully I was able to put Thomas away 7–6 (7–5) 6–2 6–2. The first set was really tight and then I got on top. Thomas served so well and hard and I think I came out with the right shots at the right time. That was the highlight of the match for me. It was one of my better matches under the circumstances.

Rain arrived at the tournament for the first time and, ominously, the forecast is not especially encouraging.

My fourth-round opponent is Boris Becker, who swept past Lleyton Hewitt 6–1 6–4 7–6 (7–5). It was a huge learning experience for Lleyton. He played his first match on centre court against one of the greatest grasscourters Wimbledon has seen.

Boris is still very dangerous. He might not be as consistent, but he retains the ability to overpower opponents and he's still a contender for the title.

Tomorrow is a rest day, but I'll head to the courts around midday for a hit, more to keep myself mentally focused than anything else. I feel as though my game is pretty much in a groove at the moment.

One of the really good things about Wimbledon this year is the number of Aussies doing well. We've got four into the fourth round — Jelena Dokic, who continues to do astonishing things after the Hingis win, Mark Philippoussis, who's really hitting his straps, and surprise packet Wayne Arthurs.

Wayne's kept a lot of the Aussie punters in the money this week. He just keeps on bombing his serve and nobody's been able to break him. The remarkable thing is that he's come through qualifying, where he won four matches, and he's now had straight-sets wins over Vincenzo Santopadre, Nicolas Lapentti and Tommy Haas to reach the round of 16.

Unfortunately for all of us, the weather is about to affect the tournament dramatically. My match with Boris doesn't get underway — and completed — until Wednesday. Perhaps it was a blessing in disguise, but the rain just didn't let up.

There's no respite from the elements, but at times like this I'm grateful that I'm renting a house close to the courts.

When Boris and I finally did make it on court, I made a bit of a slow start, but I can hardly complain about the way I played after I worked my way into the match. There was a real sense of history to the match, given the fact it was Boris's last match at Wimbledon and his final outing at Grand Slam level.

It was tough at the beginning. Boris does have a presence out there on centre court, but his game wasn't firing today and I felt like I couldn't hit the ball much better, so it wasn't a good combination for him and I won 6–3 6–2 6–3.

Boris has been one of the greatest champions Wimbledon has known and it was a pleasure to be part of his last match on centre court.

The best part was that I won.

It probably would have been better for him to finish in a bit more style, but that's the way it goes.

There was a little bit of confusion as we went to walk off, as it is obligatory to bow to the royal box if the royals are in residence.

I was looking just to walk straight off and I said to Boris, 'Do you want this occasion, because I'll just walk straight off?' and he said, 'No, no, just wait for me.' And then I'm walking off and he says, 'Hang on, you've got to bow.' Then I decided to come off court as quickly as possible and left it to Boris.

As to ending his career, I really don't care. I wanted to win and that's the way it has to be.

Boris came into the media interview-room before I did and predicted I would be among the final contenders for the Wimbledon title, but he was concerned over my doubles participation. It was an inspired comment.

For at the very time Boris was questioning the merit in my playing doubles, I was eating a quick lunch before having a shower and going out to play Lleyton Hewitt and Roger Federer. More than three hours later I'm finally off court, having survived a tough five-setter. It is not what I need at this point of a Grand Slam, let alone Wimbledon.

I've always tended to struggle at Wimbledon, but this has been a breakthrough year for me. I've finally got beyond the fourth round and I've got Todd Martin in the quarter-finals, but I'm worried about the impact doubles is having on me. I want to talk to Jonas, but it's a difficult subject to broach.

Mentally, I feel fine and there's an interesting trend emerging. I've tended to have some pretty comfortable results halfway through Grand Slams and the Enqvist and Becker results fall into that category.

At the US Open in the past, I've had those sorts of results, so it's looking good so far. The weather is still a bit patchy. I'm due to play Martin on Thursday but, by the time the weather clears, it's Friday and, as fate would have it, hot and dry.

As with all my matches against Todd, this was a difficult one. Usually my serve is one of my strengths and I really didn't have it today. I was really frustrated and Todd came up with some excellent shots. He's a great sportsman and it was something I really appreciated today.

There were some pretty ordinary calls out on court and it was hard not to feel sorry for him after beating him 6–3 6–7 (5–7) 7–6 (7–5) 7–6 (7–3) because he overturned a number of calls and then hit some screaming winners.

It was a topsy-turvy match and very chaotic with the umpire. I appealed twice and got overruled twice. There was no gamesmanship from Todd and, at times, it sounded like we were in the middle of a New York subway.

There was a truck going past shaped like a soft drink, playing really loud music. If that wasn't bad enough, there were these guys warming up on the court in front of us and they're giving a guy lobs. You see this ball flying up in the air and you're thinking, 'Is this coming on my court?' And there was a water tank behind us reflecting really bad light from one corner when we were returning from that side. There was a lot to deal with, but we both had to cope with it. The great thing about the match was the way Todd and I were able to rise above the difficulties.

Todd is a fantastic sportsman. He never tries to rip you off and he's the fairest bloke out there.

I pulled out of doubles straight after the Martin match. My decision to stop playing doubles at the Grand Slam was made simply to give myself the best chance of winning more singles titles.

I had made up my mind at the French Open, but I had given Jonas a commitment to play Wimbledon and I didn't want to pull out halfway through because that would be unfair.

Obviously I could have done without that five-set match against Hewitt and Federer after beating Becker in the singles.

I felt tired after beating Martin and that's why I've decided to opt out.

I think the doubles cost me at the French Open. It took away too much energy and affected my singles.

The pity is that Jonas and I make a good team.

We won the Australian Open and that was one of the highlights of my career. The thrill of winning that title was as good as winning my second US Open.

Jonas understands the situation and perhaps we can get together at the Slams again some time in the future.

It's not easy to talk to him about it, but he's cool.

Todd Martin caused something of a stir at his media conference when he insisted Sampras ought to be selected for singles in the Davis Cup for the quarter-final tie against us in a couple of weeks. Todd's incredibly generous even to consider it.

He and Jim Courier have been there the whole time for the US and, if I were in their position, there is no way I would step down. I know Jim won't, but Todd is such a gentleman. For his part, Pete continues to say he is available for doubles only.

It seems as if it's going to come down to a battle of wills. Sampras is pretty stubborn but, by the same token, Courier and Martin can be very persuasive and there is a lot riding on this tie. But back to Wimbledon.

I've got Andre Agassi next as the Aussie juggernaut continues to plough on.

Agassi, riding a huge wave of confidence, finally broke Wayne Arthurs' serve for a 6–7 (5–7) 7–6 (7–5) 6–1 6–4 win. Wayne held serve for 111 consecutive games before Andre got through him.

Mark Philippoussis turned in a huge performance to thrash Greg Rusedski 2–6 7–6 (7–4) 6–3 6–1 after two tight opening sets. The English media were all over Rusedski, who appeared to be injured late in the match.

The truth is that Flip really cranked up his game and his mindset is such that he believes he can bear out Cashy's prediction by winning the tournament. To do that, he'll have to get past Pete Sampras, who's yet to drop a set after wins over Scotty Draper, Sebastien Lareau, Danny Sapsford and Daniel Nestor.

And Jelena Dokic is also into the quarter-finals after a fantastic 6–4 6–3 win over Australian Open winner and world No. 7 Mary Pierce. Dokic's achievement is made even more notable for the fact she's playing her first Grand Slam on grass and she had to come through qualifying.

The weather has finally cleared up and the amazing thing is how quickly Wimbledon officials are able to clear the backlog of matches. The English fans are ecstatic over Tim Henman's progress. Having struggled with the pressures of competing at home, watching Tim reach the semi-finals after an epic five-set win over Jim Courier — Henman won 9–7 in the fifth — and then a tricky match against Cedric Pioline, I've got even more respect for the way he goes about things.

Tim's never been one to get carried away, which is pretty amazing considering the adulation which is heaped on him every time he wins a match.

I was hoping Henman would play Mark Philippoussis in the semis of the top half of the draw, but Flip has been cut down by a knee injury — and he was flying at the time.

He had won the first set 6–4 against Sampras and was at 15–40 in the third game of the second set on Pete's serve when he damaged the cartilage in his left knee. From watching the replays, you could immediately sense Mark was in a lot of pain.

He played out the game but it was obvious he could not continue. Mark was understandably shattered in defeat. He had struggled a touch for form coming into the tournament after losing in the first round of the French Open to Stolts and he was really on top of Pete when the injury occurred.

The match was similar in style to the third round of the 1996 Australian Open when Mark won in straight sets. Nobody will ever know if this match was headed in the same direction, but Mark was certainly in command.

Sampras told Flip as much as they shook hands.

'I dodged a bullet out there,' Sampras said afterwards. 'I told Mark he was kicking my ass.'

The semi-finalists are Pete Sampras and Tim Henman and Andre Agassi and me. The draw held up pretty well, with seven seeds reaching the quarter-finals, and considering former Wimbledon finalist Pioline made up the eight, it is easy to understand how tough the game has become.

Andre eliminated Gustavo Kuerten in the quarters and now the race for No. 1 has come down to a two-horse race between Agassi and myself.

Whoever wins our semi-final not only goes into the Wimbledon final, but also to the top of the rankings, which makes the match one of the most important in my career.

Reaching No. 1 after being so close over the past three years would be a tremendous achievement, but getting to the final of Wimbledon would overshadow it in my book.

I've always believed winning majors is the ultimate in the sport.

I'm just happy to have reached the semi-finals — and obviously I want more — so I've given the ranking little thought.

I've been No. 2 for a while and this is a great opportunity for me.

But Andre also has the opportunity to get to the Wimbledon final and I'm sure he'll be thinking more about winning the match than a ranking.

And whoever does get it won't have much time to reflect on it, simply because they will have to prepare for the Wimbledon final, which is the biggest match at the most important tournament in the world.

Because of the disruption to the schedule, the men's semi-finals are played on the Saturday, usually taken up with the women's final.

Unfortunately for Jelena Dokic, American teenager Alexandra Stevenson halts her run in the quarters 6–3 1–6 6–3 in the battle of the tournament qualifiers.

Jelena just couldn't quite get herself into the third set.

Lindsay Davenport then took care of Jana Novotna and Stevenson to reach her first Wimbledon final, where she'll play Steffi Graf, who had to survive two tough three-setters against Venus Williams and Mirjana Lucic to win a place in her ninth Wimbledon final.

Before Andre and I take to court one for our semi-final it becomes obvious both finals will have to be played on Sunday. I just hope I'm there and I really don't mind if I'm playing Pete or Tim. This is by far my best Wimbledon and now is the time to step it up even more.

Naturally I hope to come out of Wimbledon with the title and the world No. 1 ranking. That would be the perfect result and a great way to finish a tough week with all the weather interruptions.

It's not to be. Andre wins the match 7–5 7–6 (7–5) 6–2.

There is a saying in tennis that it is often a game of millimetres. I discovered that to my cost late in the first set when I had two sets points against Agassi's serve.

I narrowly missed a forehand and that was it for the match. I played very well for the first two sets and I didn't realise that was the only chance I was going to get. He never let me put pressure on him and, when I did, he came up with a better response.

He was simply too good and too strong. In fact, he totally outplayed me — again. There are times when you play Andre and you wonder how motivated he is and there are other times when you realise what a great player he is.

I came off court thinking I had given myself the best opportunity. I felt I played well, tried different things but, at the end of the day, he was just too good.

I couldn't find any inroads against him. I like to attack my opponent's second serve, but there was no way through and when Andre plays at this level, he's very difficult. In fact, if I'm playing at the top of my game and he's playing at the top of his game, I think you've got to put your money on Andre.

On leaving the club for another year, I reflect on the disappointment of losing my serve game in the third set with three pretty bad volleys. At this level, you are punished harshly for mistakes, but that's the way it has always been and always will be.

Overall, I think I've taken a step in the right direction. It's been a great tournament for me. Looking back, I'm unbelievably happy to have finally been in the semi-finals here. It would have been great to have kept going, but I ran into someone too good on the day.

After losing to Agassi, all I want to do is go out and have dinner and let my hair down a bit.

There's a fantastic Indian restaurant in the Wimbledon village called Rajdoot.

Most of the Aussies and the other players have eaten there at some time or other and I'm hanging out for a good curry.

I go down with my brothers Steve, Peter and Geoff, Geoff's girlfriend Mel, Lara and Little Killer.

Mid-evening, I really feel like kicking on and relaxing a little more.

We decide to go across the road to the Dog and Fox, the pub on the corner, but it's packed and from the moment I walk in there I'm being hit with requests for autographs.

We reluctantly decide to bag it and go home. I would have loved to have had a couple of beers to kick back, but it's not to be. Maybe next year.

As seems to be the way with Wimbledon, the final Sunday dawns bright and dry.

It is a huge day with Lindsay Davenport and Steffi Graf playing the women's final before Pete and Andre square off in the men's final.

Appropriately, the calendar shows that it is July 4, American Independence Day.

I can't remember the last time I saw Pete play that well. The match turned so quickly late in the first set and Andre basically never got a chance after having Sampras 0–40 at 3-all.

Pete served incredibly and he was back to his best in the way he moved around the court. It was very impressive.

There are days when you feel sympathy for some guys and it wasn't difficult to feel a little sorry for Andre, even though he beat me the day before in straight sets and he's just come off a win in the French Open.

Sampras played awesome tennis to win in straight sets. It was his sixth Wimbledon title, which is freakish at any time, let alone in the modern era when the depth of competition is clearly deeper.

Sampras said it all in the post-match press conference when he observed, 'I was on fire. Everything I did worked out.'

There was one point in the match when Andre ripped a backhand crosscourt and Sampras hit a diving backhand volley for a dropshot winner. All Andre could do was look skywards in amazement. There are times when you suspect Pete is playing a different sport to the rest of us.

The women's final was an upset as Davenport won 6–4 7–5. Graf announced post-match she had played her last match at Wimbledon in what became an emotional farewell on a busy afternoon for everybody.

Davenport made it a fantastic double by winning the doubles with Corina Morariu and Mahesh Bhupathi and Leander Paes did it again, winning the men's doubles against Paul Haarhuis and Jared Palmer. The Indians have certainly improved under the guidance of my old Australian coach Bob 'Nails' Carmichael.

Paes capped off a wonderful tournament by winning the mixed doubles with Lisa Raymond against Jonas Bjorkman and Anna Kournikova.

Lara and I decide to hang around in London for a couple of days. We've moved into a hotel and we're planning to get out and see a couple of bands and a couple of shows. We get to see *An Inspector Calls*. The culture in London is amazing and it would take years to absorb it all.

Unfortunately for both of us, the days pass way too quickly and it's time again to get on a plane for Bermuda.

DAVIS CUP

Boston I

PREPARATION

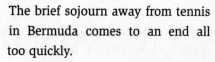

The brief sojourn away from tennis in Bermuda comes to an end all too quickly.

The Davis Cup quarter-final tie beckons in Boston and it's time to get down to some hard grind on the practice court.

Pete Sampras's form in winning his sixth Wimbledon is a bit sobering for the Aussie squad ahead of the tie this week, but we're quietly confident on the slow, gritty hardcourt the Americans have laid.

The surface was actually created to suit Jim Courier and take away some of our sting, but I don't think it's going to be Pete's perfect surface, either in singles or doubles.

It's going to be interesting in practice this week to see how Lleyton Hewitt and Andrew Ilie go in the race for the second singles place.

Lleyton is the favourite to get it, but I'm sure Andrew isn't going to hand it to him on a platter.

Whoever's successful will make their debut and it's going to be pretty tough coming up against Courier and Sampras or Todd Martin.

I remember making my debut against Russia in St Petersburg in 1994 and losing to Alexander Volkov and Yevgeny Kafelnikov.

I didn't deal with the pressures of the occasion very well. I remember feeling that not only was I playing for myself, but my teammates and my country.

I think Lleyton will definitely handle it much better than I did. He's got an incredible attitude and if he can get his teeth into the matches, he's not going to let go quickly.

And Andrew is never going to die wondering what it's like to play in the Davis Cup. Whoever gets there will do Australia proud.

The Longwood Cricket Club is about a 20-minute drive from Boston's main business district. It is a beautiful and historic old club. As with most things in Boston, which is known as the Athens of the US, the Longwood Cricket Club is the oldest of its kind in North America. Boston's history is almost overwhelming. It is the cradle of US democracy and the site of the revolution against the British. It is the spiritual home of the famous Kennedy family, the most prominent political clan in the US, and, as of this week, it has been transformed into a sporting Mecca.

The mid-season All Stars baseball game will be played at Fenway Park early next week and three days later we'll be taking on the Americans in the Davis Cup centennial tie at Longwood.

It will be 100 years to the day since Dwight Davis, a Harvard student, teamed with two university colleagues to challenge a British team. Davis donated a magnificent silver trophy, which became known as the Davis Cup.

It is arguably the finest trophy in international sport. Sweden currently holds the trophy after its victory last year but, in such a historic week, the trophy is on display at Longwood under the usual heavy security, of course.

The local media is besotted with developments in the baseball at Fenway Park. The match has been sold out for months. It pits the American League's best players against the National League's finest.

It's the perfect foil for us as we toil away in high humidity and sapping heat.

We've been splitting our days into two sessions. The morning session is usually followed by lunch at the clubhouse and, again, it is impossible not to be awestruck by the history of the place. Judging by the honour boards, Australians have excelled at Longwood.

It used to be the home of the US doubles championships when the singles championships were played at Forest Hills in New York. Australian names crop up everywhere and, even though it was a long time ago, the thought of Australians doing well here in the past gives us confidence.

According to Newk, the clubhouse is virtually unchanged from the last time he was here, which was about 1967. Neale Fraser is here this week, too, and he said the place hadn't altered a bit in 40 years.

Bud Collins, the doyen of tennis broadcasters, lives in Boston and is a Longwood member. His name also appears on the honour board, so he was obviously a pretty handy player in his time. Bud told some of the boys that the club continues to insist on an all-white dress code and that until relatively recently, black members were not permitted.

Thankfully, that particular rule has been changed but the club retains a quaint stuffiness. Despite Longwood's age, the courts are fantastic.

The grasscourts seem to go on forever. On most days it is possible to watch quartets of perfectly attired men and women playing barefooted to help protect the grass.

I'm pleased with the way my game has adapted to the hardcourt. It's medium-paced: a very fair choice when you consider the Americans wanted to lay clay. It seems to take my kick serve pretty well.

Lleyton is flying in practice and seems certain to play ahead of Andrew Ilie. There has been a hiccup in the doubles for us, though, with Todd Woodbridge's decision not to come to Boston.

Newk has known about it for a week, but has kept it secret as he tries to convince Teddy to change his mind.

It was reported that Todd had lost all his confidence after missing a couple of makeable forehands in the quarter-finals of the Wimbledon doubles against Haarhuis and Palmer.

In Newk's words, Todd doesn't know whether he can weather the storm.

Clearly we would love to have him with us. He's got a fantastic record in the Davis Cup and he's been through these kinds of confidence-troughs previously.

We'd just welcome the opportunity to help him with his confidence. The Woodies have been an integral part of our team since 1993. Todd thinks it's over; he still doesn't believe he can perform to the required level.

His absence means Australia will have a new doubles outfit for the first time since Mark Woodforde and I played and won against Croatia in Split in 1996.

The options are Mark and Sandon Stolle, Mark and me or Sandon and me.

Paul Kilderry has been seconded to the party as a hitting partner and, as usual, keeps us amused with his observations on life and his off-court antics.

The Americans remain coy over what role Sampras will play. Two things are certain, however: they want Sampras in the singles and, just as much as they want him, Sampras doesn't want to play singles. It's going to be really interesting to see what they do.

Courier will not stand aside for anybody and nor should he with his Davis Cup record, but Todd and US captain Tom Gullikson obviously feel Sampras should be in the singles mix, which is pretty understandable considering his Wimbledon achievement.

The Americans are staying in Copley Square in a hotel adjacent to ours.

On the Tuesday before the tie, the US Tennis Association rolls out the team for individual interviews.

Martin is first and makes no bones about why he thinks Pete should play.

Courier is next and firmly makes the point that, once selected, there is no room for half measures.

'Pete should not feel uncomfortable about being on the team,' says Courier.

'But once you're on, you're on. I think he should be playing singles. We want to sit down with him as a team and talk it over. I know "Gully" [Gullikson] wants it to happen too.

'I think Todd and I can be pretty persuasive.'

Sampras follows Courier and immediately makes it clear he is not happy stepping on anybody's toes. 'I've said all along I'm not comfortable coming in and playing singles,' he said. 'This is Todd's show and Jim's show. They've been there for the long haul and I don't want to be jumping on their bandwagon. I'm very sensitive to how they feel.'

Gullikson sat on the fringes of the media pack listening to what he probably did not want to hear. The US resolved to discuss the issue over dinner.

Earlier that day Pete had walked onto court at the end of the Australian practice session. Since it was my first opportunity to personally congratulate him on the Wimbledon win, I did so. It was a phenomenal effort.

And, as much as we strive to beat each other out on court, once the match is over, you should be able to look your opponent in the eye and say 'well played' and move on.

Life is far too short to hold grudges or to begrudge anybody success.

There have been times when I've been annoyed at the timing and intent of some of Pete's remarks, but there's no question he's been the best player of the decade.

His record emphatically proves that and it's precisely the reason the Americans want him to play singles.

Outside of Sampras, the most important factor here is the weather. When we arrived late last week, it was extremely pleasant. A week on, it is hot and humid. We have to be careful to rehydrate properly, especially as Rochey and Newk go out of their way to make sure we're going to be in top form by the time the tie starts.

The draw is set down for tomorrow. Word slips out that Sampras won't be talked into playing singles, meaning I'll play Jim Courier on the first day, with Lleyton to debut against Todd Martin. The Americans are going to field Sampras and Alex O'Brien in the doubles.

We're likely to go with Mark Woodforde and Sandon Stolle, who've been burning in practice.

A dinner tonight merely confirms our suspicions over Sampras. He's not keen at all to be involved in anything but the doubles.

The draw is held on the lawns of the Longwood Cricket Club. Both teams are required to assemble inside the clubhouse, in uniform, and then file down opposite sides of the verandah at the front of the building.

As usual, there is a lot of pomp attached to the ceremony, not least of which is because of the presence of a stack of retired Australian and US Davis Cup players.

Frank Sedgman, Ken McGregor, Allan Stone and John Fitzgerald are there for us, along with Newk and Rochey. The American contingent is much larger, of course. Among the notables is Jack Kramer, who is regarded by many Americans as the father of professional tennis.

After a series of short speeches, the draw pans out almost perfectly for us.

Lleyton is drawn to play Todd in the first match, followed by me playing Jim.

Newk settled on Pecker and Sandon for the doubles. They'll play Sampras and O'Brien. As it stands right now, I'll play Martin in the first of the reverse singles on Sunday, leaving Lleyton to play Courier in the fifth rubber.

By now everybody is tense, but there are duties still to be taken care of.

Both teams attend the last of the pre-match interviews.

Sampras seems annoyed at persistent questioning over his decision to bypass singles.

'Well, I wasn't lying when I told you that,' he said. 'I've been saying it for three months and I've never changed my position.'

Gullikson, by all accounts, was just as annoyed with the line of questioning, which was immediately siezed upon by Newk when we showed up for our media conference.

Drawing on a lifetime of experience, Newk said he would not like to be in Gully's position if they happened to lose with Pete sitting on the sidelines, and also predicted the US could not afford for Martin to lose to Lleyton.

We eventually escaped to the practice court for last-minute fine-tuning.

But there's not much you can do at this point. If you're not ready, you're not going to recover in 24 hours.

It doesn't matter how many Davis Cup ties you've played — you are still as nervous as hell the night before a tie. This one is no exception. There is so much riding on it. We didn't want the tie played here and the Americans know it.

There is a huge media contingent in town for the match. Courier and Martin's efforts in Birmingham against Britain have really captured the imagination of the Americans. And the Longwood membership is not backward in supporting their players, either.

As we hit the sack tonight, we know tomorrow is going to be a huge day.

Boston II

MATCH TIME

The first match is vitally important. If Lleyton can get us off to a good start, there's a reasonable chance we can be 2–0 by the end of the first day's play.

It quickly became obvious Lleyton had been ready to play Davis Cup tennis for a long time, but nobody knew just how ready he was.

His game is perfectly suited to the Davis Cup, and so is his temperament.

And he showed it all against Todd Martin. Watching the match on television from the locker-room, it was difficult not to get excited.

I know how tough Todd is to play, but Lleyton matched him really well.

And with the conditions being so brutal, you had to put your money on Lleyton over five sets.

He was totally unfazed by the circumstances, while Todd seem to suffer in the heat. There were small signs early on that Todd was going to struggle. A double fault in the opening game at 40–0 seems insignificant in the overall scheme of things, but it showed that, despite all his experience, Todd was also feeling the pressure.

Lleyton didn't take long to get into the match. He was under the pump at 0–40 in the fourth game of the match, but eased his way out of it and then broke Martin's serve to lead 3–2. If Todd had suspected he was in for a long day, he certainly knew it when Lleyton won the first set after 43 minutes.

Martin realised the match could slip away quickly unless he dug in and won the second set and he broke serve to lead 2–0. Lleyton got it back to 1–2, and the match went with serve to the tiebreak, where Todd really cranked it up to win it 7–1.

With the match level, it was going to come down to who took their chances.

The amazing thing about Lleyton was how well he handled the situation. There was so much riding on the first match, yet there was never a hint of anxiety when he ripped a forehand down the line to break for 4–2. It was a huge moment.

From that moment on, Todd won only one more game for the match. Lleyton gave up only nine points in the fourth set as the capacity crowd sat silently contemplating the birth of a Davis Cup star.

Lleyton has been waiting in the wings, watching the older guys at practice and in matches since he was 15. He's only just turned 18 now, but he's a hell of a player.

The pressures of Davis Cup tennis do strange things to players. Some guys revel in it, others are stifled by it. Lleyton loves it. He loves the big occasion and he really does thrive on it. There are very few players in the world with a similar mentality.

It was incredible sitting there watching him work Todd over. I think Todd realised early on that Lleyton wouldn't be going away in a hurry. And we all knew that once he got his teeth into the match, he would be very difficult to overcome.

It is amazing how it's turned out for him. Two weeks ago, he was coming to Boston, in his own mind, probably as the fifth player. I thought all along he had a great chance of playing.

But when Mark Philippoussis hurt his knee at Wimbledon, the door opened for him. He had enough time to get nervous, and I'm sure he was, but he handled the situation beautifully. The fact he was playing a world-class opponent in front of a hostile audience and the Australian Prime Minister, John Howard, had no effect on him at all.

Lleyton put us on the right track with his 6–4 6–7 (1–7) 6–3 6–0 win and now it was up to me to nail the advantage.

I knew Jim was going to be tough. He revels in adversity and he knows how to whip the crowd into hysteria.

Knowing Lleyton had put us in a great position was strange in a way. I had to try and control myself absorbing his win and I tried to be as relaxed as I could. I probably felt too relaxed in the beginning but, in the end, I think that worked in my favour because I didn't want to get too hyped up. You can drain a lot of energy out there.

The match was predictably tight and then we played a very strange tiebreak, considering we were holding our serve quite comfortably. But in the tiebreak, it was sort of swinging around so I thought I was on top, then he was on top.

It was a comedy of unforced errors until I got a good first serve in. I think we were both trying to give that tiebreak away there for a while.

Jim had two serves to come when he led 5–4, but then he hit a forehand and two backhands long to give me the set.

There was only one break of serve for 5–4 in the second set and the third set was pretty tight until Jim got a pretty ordinary line-call to drop his serve at 5–4 in the third set.

I started getting some good momentum on my serves and I just tried to put as much pressure on Jim as I could. I worked hard for the break in the second set and then in the third set, he had a very bad line-call.

In fact, we both had some bad line-calls at really crucial times.

His call turned out to be more crucial than mine.

Throughout the match there was also an orange blimp hovering over the site.

Its engine would cut out and then restart and after a while it really seemed to get on Jim's nerves. He made his feelings very clear and I don't blame him.

I guess it was a bit like the promotional drinks truck at Wimbledon.

I was eventually able to walk off court with a 7–6 (7–5) 6–4 6–4 win.

The conditions were brutal out there. I know it was hot during Lleyton's match, but it felt twice as hot for the match with Courier.

I was just trying to pace myself, thinking I could have a five-set match. It was a matter of trying to lift my game and assert myself when it really mattered. If I didn't win the first two points of Jim's service game or one out of the first three, then I just let the game go.

It was the only way of tackling the match in the conditions.

Initially I didn't think I was competing that well from the baseline but, as the match wore on, I felt more comfortable. Jim was going for that big forehand and some of my backhands just had nothing on them, so it was probably hard for Jim to generate pace.

I didn't mean to hit them that badly, but it was like what Felix Mantilla said in Rome about me when he reckoned his grandmother hit it harder than me.

The feeling of leading 2–0 after the first day is huge. It's not going to get any better than this. As we leave Longwood for our downtown hotel, we know we're going to have a great dinner, a few drinks and a chat about finishing the job tomorrow.

We're all desperate to get that third point to win the tie. And we want to take the uncertainty out of it all by cleaning it up 3–0.

You can't underestimate the US. They could easily get back into the tie and win it 3–2. Hopefully, we'll shut them out in the doubles.

I've told Newk I'm available if he needs me. We can change the team up until an hour before the doubles.

Newk says he has got to weigh up the pros and cons of playing me again tomorrow before the reverse singles on Sunday.

His basic dilemma is knowing how well Mark Woodforde and I played against Croatia three years ago and also the way Sandon Stolle and I went at the World Team Cup in Dusseldorf.

Newk has to decide whether to go for broke tomorrow with me or choose to go with Pecker and Sandon, who are a perfectly good team, as shown by their outstanding practice form.

We chat about it over dinner and everybody is in high spirits.

Eventually we decide that Pecker and Sandon are the guys who should play the doubles. That way Lleyton and I will have rested ahead of the reverse singles.

The Americans are under the pump. The spectators are openly questioning Sampras's decision to bypass singles. Newk put it succinctly when he said: 'We are in the fortunate position of having our opposition on the ropes'.

The tie has occupied our minds for the past ten days, but the occasion has been overshadowed by the tragic accident involving John F. Kennedy Jnr, his wife Carolyn and sister-in-law Lauren. The accident, in a light plane, claimed all three lives and it happened not far south of Boston.

Some of the retired players went to a lavish function at the John F. Kennedy Presidential Library and Museum on Friday night when the Kennedy plane plunged into the sea.

The building is full of Kennedy memorabilia, including photographs of the assassinated President playing with his son.

From what we would learn later, the accident occurred about the time the 70 former players were being presented on stage in front of ITF officials. I think everyone felt a bit numb.

Once we got to the courts, the focus returned immediately to the job in hand. There was a pre-match scare for us when Sandon walked straight into a girder in the locker-room, belting his head in the process. The really strange thing was that Sandon was unaware of the extent of the injury. It wasn't until he walked out to the practice court that he noticed blood on his cap. There was more, by this stage, trickling down his forehead, and it took the medical staff ten minutes to stop the bleeding.

The incident is typical of what Davis Cup pressure can do. Some players thrive on it, others go into a trance and produce outstanding tennis and others are stifled by it.

Sandon won a dead singles rubber against France in Sydney two years ago, but this match is incredibly important.

Sampras is clearly pumped for the occasion, although a double fault on the opening point of the match betrays a few nerves.

Strange as it seems to say of a match that eventually wound on for five long sets, the third game of the first set was crucial.

Alex O'Brien, with more than a little help from Sampras, saved four break points in a really tense opening. From that moment on, O'Brien appeared more comfortable on court as the scratch US team began to combine better.

The American crowd was unbelievably loud. There is a partisan rule in Davis Cup in which supporters of the host nation and sometimes those following the visiting country can draw penalties on the players because of unfair barracking.

Tennis etiquette is observed more closely in some countries than others.

In Australia and England, for instance, it is abnormal for the crowd to clap or cheer double faults. The same goes for unforced errors.

But when national pride is at stake during a centennial tie, emotions tend to run high. When Sandon served at 4–5 at the end of the first set and found himself down 0–40, the call of 'break, break' was deafening.

At those times, it is almost impossible to hear, let alone think clearly.

Unfortunately for Sandon, he double-faulted on set point and the crowd went berserk.

The noise level hardly abated over the next 40 minutes as the Americans surged to a two-sets-to-love lead after Pecker dropped serve for 2–4 when Sampras cracked a forehand winner. Pecker and Sandon were obviously in real strife, but they refused to cave in.

Newk urged them to persist and slowly the match began to turn. They broke O'Brien's serve for 5–3 in the third set and then Pecker served it out. Suddenly, there was a bit of tension among the crowd.

Things would quickly get worse for the Americans when Sampras dropped his serve in the opening game of the fourth set. We had a chance to break O'Brien's serve in the third game, but the boys were on a roll.

They almost broke Sampras again at 4–5 for the set, but couldn't quite pull out. But when Pecker served out the fourth set, the match and possibly the tie could hang on the fifth rubber.

The crowd by this stage was almost hysterical, having yelled itself hoarse.

Games went with serve until the eighth game, when Pecker again found himself under the crushing weight of Cup pressure.

The guys twice had game point, but could not seal it. Eventually Sampras and O'Brien created a break point as the game wound on for a good eight minutes. Then came the point of the match, possibly the tie, which ended with a Woodforde smash at the tail of a huge rally. There was a deserved standing ovation for both teams. Unfortunately for Mark and Sandon, the Americans persisted. Mark, having saved another break point with a fantastic second-serve ace down the middle, brought up a third break point with his third double fault of the game.

Sandon had the misfortune of hitting a backhand long and the Americans were beside themselves with joy. All that remained now was for Sampras to serve out the game and the match.

That he almost stumbled was an appropriate punctuation mark to an amazing match. Sandon and Mark somehow composed themselves for one last fling at the match and had Sampras down 30–40 before Sampras asserted himself.

The Americans finally eased to a 6–4 6–3 3–6 4–6 6–3 win in three hours and 27 minutes.

Suddenly, the tie was alive again. Our mood was less buoyant as we made our way back to the hotel.

Inside the media tent another drama was unfolding, as Todd Martin practised on the match court.

Unbeknown to Martin, Gullikson and Sampras were openly discussing the merits of a possible substitution. Martin was in danger of being replaced and didn't know it.

He had discussed the issue with Gullikson the previous night and was convinced he would be playing me in the fourth rubber and was carrying on with his preparations.

But Gullikson refused to rule it out as Sampras said that all options had to be considered. Trouble was, they forgot to tell Todd and he was far from impressed when told by an Australian reporter that Gullikson was considering the move.

The following day brought one of the most eventful interludes in my career.

Boston III

DECIDING MATCH

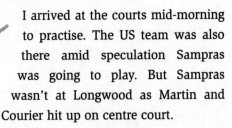

I arrived at the courts mid-morning to practise. The US team was also there amid speculation Sampras was going to play. But Sampras wasn't at Longwood as Martin and Courier hit up on centre court.

The drama started about 11 am. Todd had practised and felt dizzy.

He returned to the US locker-room, sat in front of a mirror and immediately realised he was in trouble.

I had been on court for just 15 minutes and I felt myself dehydrating.

The humidity was utterly sapping and it took a lot of energy just to move, let alone to keep the body cool.

Todd sought out Gullikson but couldn't find him.

What followed was one of the most tumultous hours in the history of tennis relations between Australia and the US.

Martin was firstly assessed as being unfit to play by Dr David Altchek, the ATP Tour's leading doctor and the medico who operated on Mark Philippoussis's left knee in New York the previous week.

Knowing Todd, there is no way he would have been faking. Martin was then examined by the neutral doctor, longtime Longwood Cricket Club member, Rich Paul.

Dr Paul agreed with Altchek and told the Swedish referee Stefan Fransson.

Fransson then summoned Newk to a hastily convened meeting as Gullikson frantically attempted to contact Sampras to come down to the club to get ready.

To say Newk was unimpressed by the decision is to understate matters substantially. He was furious.

He told Fransson and Paul that if Todd was not well enough to play because of the amount of fluid he had lost during the warm-up, then I was in the same predicament.

He pointed out in very basic Australian vernacular the way he felt the whole situation had been handled before storming back into the Australian locker-room.

By this stage, I didn't know who I was playing.

Was it Martin or was it Sampras? It was becoming ridiculous. I needed to know who I should be preparing for. At this stage it was after midday and less than an hour before match-time.

Newk returned to the referee's office and teed off again. By now it was less than half an hour until the match was due to start. Newk bluntly reminded those present of the need for integrity.

Eventually sanity prevailed and Todd was ordered to play.

When Todd and I walked out on court, it was obvious he didn't look great. It was later revealed he had attempted to come into our locker-room to convince us that he was serious about the way he was feeling.

To this day, we have no doubt he was ailing. I think he became a victim of the cat-and-mouse tactics some of the other people around him were playing. I think if we hadn't been 2–1 up and there hadn't been so much discussion over the possibility of Sampras replacing him, we might have been more accommodating.

But the rules are the rules. Dr Paul overturned his original assessment and a potentially nasty incident was averted.

I sympathised with Todd as we hit up because I could see he was very pale.

In those circumstances, it can be difficult to stay focused and this was no exception.

Todd came out swinging. He broke my serve in the first game and again in the third game. He still didn't look great, but he was pulling winners from everywhere.

There was a point early in the fifth game of the first set when the US support staff were urging Gullikson to get Todd off court. I'm not sure whether I imagined it or not, but I thought he was staggering around out there.

Todd's mother was understandably concerned. At one stage, she was heard calling out, 'I want my son alive after this match.' Emotions were clearly running high in the US support box. Todd's girlfriend was in tears and there were a number of fierce glares directed at the Aussie contingent. I tried to put it all out of my mind as I struggled to get the upper hand over Todd. I knew I had to stay with him because of the difficulty he was having in the conditions, but as Todd worked himself into the match, I knew I was in a lot of trouble.

Once a sick or injured player gets a ball in their zone and they're relaxed, they tend to go for everything. My plan was to get up early in the first set and make him feel as badly as I could.

Unfortunately for me, Todd's plan was to keep the points as short as possible and everything was working for him.

I tried to get a few first serves in and, boom, there were winners all over the place. He didn't really give me a chance to get nervous in the beginning. My goal was to win this match and take the fifth rubber out of the equation.

As well as Lleyton had played against Todd on Friday, I didn't want him to have to go out and play Jim in the fifth match if it was still a live rubber. This was the most crucial match of the tie and Martin was on a huge roll.

He whipped through the first set in 33 minutes before we swapped service breaks in the third and fourth games of the second set. I then had him down 0–40 at 2–3 and couldn't capitalise. Everything I tried seemed to be fractionally off.

Everything Todd attempted worked.

It was as simple as that and the doubts were starting to creep in.

Worse was to follow at 5–5 when Todd mis-hit a backhand return — one of his most dangerous shots — and then nailed a rocketing backhand return down the line for the break.

He then served out the set and had the jubilant US cheer squad on its feet.

It was crunch time.

I was desperate for a good start in the third set. My adrenalin and energy levels were still very high and I knew if I could get through the next couple of sets, then I could beat him. As brilliantly as Todd returns, and as well as he serves, Todd gets on streaks and you just have to weather the storm.

His winners were coming from all angles and I just didn't know what to do. I had to convince myself to keep playing my game, perhaps change one or two little things, but when it comes down to the nitty gritty, you have got to put your game up against his and see who comes out on top.

The first game of the third set was critical. For me, in this instance, it teetered on the brink of disaster.

The very first point of the game set the standard. I lobbed Todd and, despite his obviously less-than-perfect condition, he scampered back and hit what was later described as a circus shot — a whipped forehand down the line — as he rotated 180 degrees. I have rarely seen a ball travel as quickly through the air.

The crowd went mad. They were happy soon after when I hit a pair of double faults to slump to 15–40. Things were by now very grim. I conjured an ace from somewhere, scrambled back to deuce and held on to win the game.

I felt I had taken the first step up the mountain, but it was still a long haul and I was not out of the woods yet, not by a long shot.

I broke and led 4–1, before Todd again dug in. I had the chance to break his serve for the set, but he foiled me and then had me down 15–40 at 5–3 as I attempted to serve out the set. Eventually I did and I sensed the momentum swing.

Todd would have been inhuman not to feel discouraged, but I was trying not to think about him too much. He sat under an umbrella at the changeovers hidden under three wet towels. From what I could tell, Gullikson was not saying too much to him, preferring to let Todd recover.

It was during this phase of the match that I remember asking Newk to have a word with the umpire to keep an eye on how much time Todd was taking at the changeovers. He's a close friend of mine, and I knew he wasn't feeling well, but I didn't want to be handing him an advantage by letting something like that slip.

As I've said before, you won't find a finer sportsman than Todd. There's no way he'd try and cheat me deliberately, but every second is vital on the changeovers. You've got 90 seconds to sit down, cool off as much as you can, drink what you need and take in the advice your captain has to offer.

I felt Todd's intensity was beginning to wane.

The first signs came in the opening game of the set when I got him down 30–40, but couldn't put him away. I got him four games later when he netted a couple of backhand volleys and I jogged to the chair just to let the opposition player, captain, support group and the crowd know that I wasn't going to go away.

I broke Todd's serve to lead 5–2 two games later when he punched a backhand volley wide and then levelled at two sets all.

I felt much more confident about my game and I thought the momentum was continuing to flow my way. Todd had an entirely different view.

I had been heckled by some people in the crowd during the first set and was pretty annoyed in the second game of the fifth set. Martin hit a forehand crosscourt return winner for 15–30 and then I nudged a forehand long to be down 15–40.

My mood was not helped at all when a spectator with nothing better to do deliberately rattled a can between my first and second serves. Todd took advantage and smacked a backhand return down the line to lead 2–0.

His lead soon ballooned to 3–0 and obviously there was a fair bit of concern.

But I know I'm always going to get my chance against Todd. The only worry was how long he could maintain the streak.

If he kept it up, there was a good chance I was going to walk off court a loser and the tie would be squared up at 2–2.

With a lot of help from Newk and all the boys on the sidelines I stayed positive. I reminded myself that I had won ten five-set matches in a row and memories of those wins were the foundation of what was about to unfold.

Something picks me up when I get into a five-setter and, although I'm down, I know I can go out there and still accomplish what I have to accomplish. I know I'm going to be the last one out there. My body might not want to last, but my mind and everything else wants me to keep going.

I knew I had to break Todd's serve quickly and I hauled myself back into it when he pushed a backhand volley long to drop serve for 3–2.

Having worked my butt off to get the match back on serve, I played a really bad game to lose serve for 2–4 when I double-faulted, hit a backhand volley long and then Todd hit a forehand winner down the line.

I completed the disaster by hitting a backhand half volley long and Todd had the upper hand.

The seventh game suddenly became the most important game of my life. I had to get back on terms or the match was probably lost. Todd made a couple of volley errors and then double-faulted. Again I felt the tide was turning.

Thankfully, my instinct was right.

I held serve to love and broke Todd's serve to lead 5–4 with my serve to come.

It was a moment of total exhilaration. I played a couple of shots in that game that weren't really my style, but I came up with them. It was the high point of the match for me when I broke his serve.

I ran across to the sidelines and everybody was on their feet. On the other side of the net, there were downcast expressions everywhere. I think back now about the forehand down the line I played. It is not a shot I'm entirely comfortable with, and it almost came out of nowhere, but suddenly I was serving for the match.

The game went really quickly. The crowd did its best to lift Todd, who now found himself down three match points after three hours and 14 minutes in some of the most gruelling conditions I've encountered.

The elation I felt when he hit a backhand long was almost indescribable.

After shaking hands with Todd, Newk and Gullikson, I went over to the boys to share the moment. The Fanatics, led by Warren Livingston, had been fantastic. All of a sudden, I found myself hoisted on the shoulders of Paul Kilderry and Lleyton Hewitt.

Walking off court after winning 4–6 5–7 6–3 6–2 6–4 and helping put us 3–1 ahead and into the semi-finals against Russia was one of the most joyous occasions I've had so far in my career. I'm sure it's going to take a couple of days to sink in.

My body is pretty battered. I felt fine physically on court, but I was mentally rattled at the start of the match. Now it's the opposite. I spent 20 minutes or so hobbling around on the adjacent grasscourts with Muddy Waters and Rochey.

Eventually I made my way to the media conference, where the press continued to give Gullikson a real going-over.

There were suggestions he ought to stand down from his job, but he was vehemently defended by Sampras, who said the only reason he had returned to the Davis Cup fold was because of Gullikson. Sampras had been coached by Gullikson's twin brother, Tim, who died of brain cancer in 1996.

With the tie safely in our keeping, it was simply a matter of being able to enjoy. Lleyton put the icing on the cake with a 7–5 6–4 win over Alex O'Brien, who stood in for Jim Courier.

True to form, Lleyton was totally unaffected by the fact that this was a dead rubber. He attacked the match with his usual intensity and aggression.

Even when O'Brien led 4–2 in the second set, Lleyton would not be discouraged.

To win 4–1 against arguably the most powerful nation in tennis on their home ground was obviously a huge achievement for us.

It had been 26 years since Australia had last won against the US in the United States.

It was back in 1973, incidentally, that Australia posted a 5–0 win in Cleveland. The Australian team was composed of Rod Laver, Ken

Rosewall, Mal Anderson and Newk. Laver and Newk played all five matches under Neale Fraser.

So there was a real sense of history about what had occurred in Boston.

One of the most enjoyable aspects of the tie at Longwood Cricket Club this week has been the camaraderie among the past and present Davis Cup players — Australian and American.

And although we were opposed to the US being given the privilege of holding the tie at Longwood, everything worked out perfectly. In the overall scheme of things, Longwood was the appropriate venue.

There is a great Australian heritage running through it.

Australians have had enormous success here over the years and some of them had returned this week for the centennial tie.

Frank Sedgman, Ken McGregor and Neale Fraser all played here and achieved a lot during their prime and they'd managed to come over from Australia for this match.

They were among some of the greatest players we've ever had and it was a thrill to pose for a photograph with them in front of the clubhouse.

After a brief celebration at Longwood, interrupted briefly by Jim Courier's visit to our rooms to offer his congratulations, we returned to the hotel for a serious party.

There was the traditional post-tie dinner where, as is the great Australian custom, those in attendance were required to don napkins on their heads.

It was a fantastic occasion and the speeches were priceless.

As usual, Little Killer's offering brought the house down. In between the mirth, there was a lot of seriousness as we reflected on reaching the semi-final stage.

I made a speech to thank everybody on the team, but especially Rochey.

He's a fantastic coach and he's been largely responsible for my success. More than that, he's a tremendous friend and a top bloke.

Patrolling
the net,
Heineken
Trophy.

BORIS BECKER BIDDING FAREWELL TO THE WIMBLEDON CROWD FOR
THE LAST TIME AFTER I BUNDLED HIM OUT IN STRAIGHT SETS.

TOP: GREY SKIES
WERE A CONSTANT
COMPANION DURING
THE 1999 ALL
ENGLAND LAWN
TENNIS
CHAMPIONSHIPS AT
WIMBLEDON. HERE
I AM ON COURT 3
WITH MY DOUBLES
PARTNER JONAS
BJORKMAN OF
SWEDEN.

RIGHT: TODD
MARTIN PUSHED
ME TO THE EDGE
IN OUR QUARTER-
FINAL AT
WIMBLEDON.
ALWAYS THE
CONSUMMATE
SPORTSMAN,
TODD OVERTURNED
A NUMBER OF POOR
UMPIRING CALLS —
TO MY ADVANTAGE
— BUT WENT DOWN
IN FIVE TOUGH
SETS.

CHANGING
SWEATBANDS.

ANDRE AGASSI'S
RETURN TO THE TOP
FLIGHT HAS BEEN
NOTHING SHORT OF
PHENOMENAL. HE
CRUSHED ME IN THE
SEMI-FINAL AT
WIMBLEDON, BUT
MET A RED-HOT
PETE SAMPRAS IN
THE FINAL.

THE FANATICS IN THE STANDS AT LONGWOOD CRICKET CLUB FOR THE ENERGY-SAPPING DAVIS CUP QUARTER-FINAL AGAINST THE UNITED STATES. THEIR COLOURFUL ANTICS WERE A WELCOME SIDESHOW ON THE ATP TOUR.

MY FIVE-SET DAVIS CUP VICTORY OVER TODD MARTIN WAS ONE OF THE MOST JOYOUS MOMENTS IN MY ENTIRE CAREER, DESPITE ALL THE PRE-MATCH DRAMAS. THE WIN CLINCHED THE TIE AND PUT AUSTRALIA INTO THE SEMIS AGAINST RUSSIA.

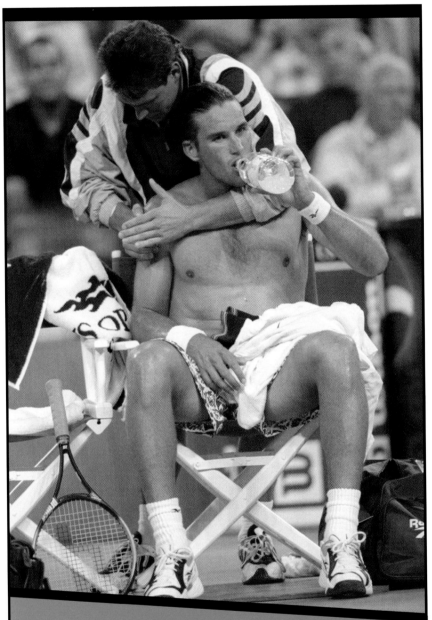

DESPITE TREATMENT ON MY SHOULDER BETWEEN SETS IN MY FIRST-ROUND CLASH WITH FRENCHMAN CEDRIC PIOLINE AT THE 1999 US OPEN, I KNEW I WAS GOING TO MAKE AN EARLY EXIT.

BOWING OUT OF THE LAST MAJOR OF 1999,

MY DREAM OF A THIRD CONSECUTIVE US OPEN VICTORY WAS
SHATTERED. THE BOOS FROM THE CROWD DIDN'T HELP EASE
THE PAIN.

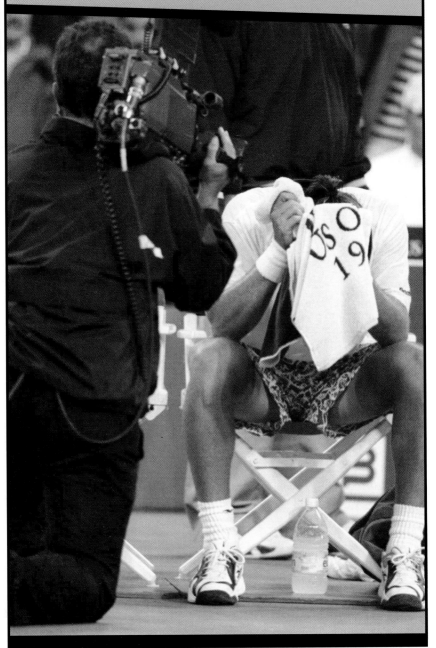

To have Rochey and Newk on the sidelines is a huge boost for the current group of Australian players. And hopefully what we learn from them over time will be passed onto the young players coming up now.

Lleyton, Mark Philippoussis, Andrew Ilie and myself are very fortunate to have this kind of exposure. The Woodies, Jason Stoltenberg and Scotty Draper have played their best tennis since their appointment.

There is nothing coincidental about the fact Australian tennis has come on in leaps and bounds since Newk and Rochey became more closely involved with us.

As dinner winds down, we decide to kick on for a party at one of a string of Irish pubs in Boston. Clary's has become well known to 'Wozza' (Warren Livingston) during his search for members of the Fanatics.

The best thing is that it's only 100 metres from our hotel, which is probably a good thing considering the revelry which was to follow.

Predictably, Kilderry was the star of the show. He marshalled the drinking games, the singing and the general organisation of the impromptu party.

The highpoint came late in the evening when he was challenged to strip. He duly obliged, shedding most of his clothes, but mercifully stopped short of going all the way.

The really interesting thing was that there was a group of American girls in Clary's who had conspicuously, and very loudly, supported the US during the tie.

Now they were leading the cheers for Kilderry and slipping dollar bills into the back of his jocks.

It was a tremendous party. The guys from the Fanatics were very funny.

Kilderry was described at the dinner as 'the best No. 6 on the Australian team' we had ever had. It was pretty hard to disagree.

Everybody at Clary's had a good time, ranging from Geoff Pollard, the president of Tennis Australia, to the players to the complete strangers who chose to join in.

In the middle of all the happiness, though, something was not quite right and it wasn't until the morning that we found out why.

Our fantastic win took on a completely different complexion on Monday morning when the players were told of the death of Scott Draper's wife Kellie.

Kel's death was kept secret from us by Newk, but I suspect Mark Woodforde knew about it. Pecker didn't stay late at the celebrations last night.

Newk went home early, too.

It is devastating for all us close to Kel and Scotty.

We all knew Kel wasn't well because she made regular visits to hospital due to cystic fibrosis, but no-one intruded into the Drapers' situation. We respected their privacy.

It turned out that Kel died at the time we were playing the reverse singles. Sue Roche knew of it, but swore herself to secrecy. It is a very sad time for all us.

Jason Stoltenberg was very close to Kel and Scotty and he's going to fly home for the funeral service.

I spoke to Scott and he was incredibly positive about the situation.

He's grateful that he had the time he had with Kel, which is a really brave way of looking at things.

Kel's Dad, John, has also been very impressive in the way he's handled it.

Kel was a wonderful friend to all of us and she'll be sadly missed.

With Kel's passing and the deaths of John Kennedy and Carolyn and Lauren Bessette, it really hits home hard that you should try to make the most of every day.

I've got some commercial obligations to fulfil this week and I'm going over to Salem, scene of the infamous witchcraft trials, to play a round of golf.

For all the distractions, it is impossible to get the Davis Cup out of my mind. The victory was one of the great experiences of my career so far. To win 4–1 on US home soil in front of a really rough crowd was fantastic.

Everybody played their part. Lleyton Hewitt made a great debut, Sandon Stolle and Pecker were unlucky not to win a tough five-setter and I was happy with the way I played.

We all realise now what a great opportunity we have to win the Cup this year. We've got Russia at home, with the chance to play France or Belgium in the final. I'd love to see the tie against Russia played in Brisbane, but we need to get all the players together and work out what's best for all of us.

We want to get the right surface and the right ball. We'll take all of that into consideration to give us the best chance of making sure we get to the final.

We might not have a better opportunity than this.

Boston IV

CELEBRATIONS

One of the last things I did before leaving Boston was to be presented with a trophy from Newk made of Waterford Crystal, marking my imminent rise to No. 1 in the world rankings. I've known for a couple of weeks that I would probably take over from Andre Agassi on Monday if everything fell the way the ATP Tour expected.

The presentation was a fantastic moment for both of us. It was especially significant that Newk should make the presentation. Newk was the first Australian to reach No. 1 on the computer rankings back in 1974.

As much as I had contemplated becoming No. 1 over the past couple of years, Newk had been pushing for it to happen as well. There are some people in sport or business who can never let go of the past. Newk is not one of them. Like everybody else around Australian tennis, Newk is thrilled for me.

It has become a bit of a tradition for the ATP Tour to commission a No. 1 ranking trophy for the newest recipient and have it presented by someone appropriate. The trophy was designed by Italian artist Celano Giannici and it will take pride of place at my home.

Growing up in Mount Isa, I never dreamed I would become the No. 1 tennis player in the world. In fact, I can't even remember joking about it as a kid, but it's true, I will become No. 1 next week when the new rankings are released.

I've got mixed feelings about it all. I don't quite understand what the fuss is about. To me, at this point of my career when there is hopefully a lot left ahead of me, it is almost insignificant. Getting to No. 1 is not as important to me as winning Grand Slams.

But, at the same time, it is obviously very nice to be able to say that I have got to No.1, regardless of how long I can hang onto the ranking.

I'll be the fifth different No. 1 this year — behind Pete Sampras, Yevgeny Kafelnikov, Carlos Moya and Andre Agassi — and the 17th No. 1 since the computer rankings system was introduced in 1973. Newk is the only other Australian to have reached No. 1, so that's a feather in my cap.

There's a historical significance to reaching No. 1 that I'm sure I'll appreciate much more when my career is over.

When I first started out on the Tour, the rankings meant a lot more. I would come up against a highly ranked player and be desperate to get the bonus points for beating them because every rankings point in those days was like gold.

As time wore on, you might come up against Pete Sampras but you wouldn't think about the bonus points you might collect if you were successful. You would just recognise him as a great player, which is the ultimate accolade.

To finally reach No. 1 is fulfilling in the sense that I've been close to achieving it so often. Twice this year I've gone on court, in the Italian Open final against Gustavo Kuerten and the Wimbledon semi-final against

Andre Agassi, knowing I would go to No. 1 if I won the match. It didn't happen on either occasion.

I have no special celebrations planned for tomorrow. I had a few extra beers a couple of weeks ago when it became apparent I could go to No. 1 during the next week.

Being No. 1 is going to make me a larger target for some players but I'm used to that kind of pressure, too, having been at No. 2 for a couple of years now. Obviously there is a lot of competition and plenty of ambitious players wanting to take a shot at me.

Right now, I'm happy to say I've got to No. 1, but I want more Slams.

From what I can tell, there is quite a lot of excitement about the ranking back in Australia. My family has taken a lot of telephone calls and they're obviously very thrilled.

It's great that they can be involved in this because their sacrifices are part of the reason I've been able to have a tennis career. They've gone without a lot of things just so I could have a shot at making it.

I remember being allowed to have my own room as a kid because I needed to have a good night's sleep, and my family drove me all over Queensland to compete in junior tournaments. Without them, I would not have reached No. 1. They've given me incredible support. There's Mum and Dad, Jocelyn and Jim, and there's Steve, Theresa, Geoff, Marie, Peter, Louise, Michael and David. As far as I know, we're the biggest family on the international circuit.

They've never given up on me. I was never a star as a kid and Paul Kilderry, who beat me eight times in a row as a junior, remarked recently that if he had lost to me at that stage of our respective careers, he would have regarded it as a bad loss.

My game took a lot of work. I was a serve-volleyer and it's the hardest game for a kid to play, but I never gave up on it and part of the reason for my persistence was my family's faith in me.

There were some pretty tough times for me as a junior when I couldn't break into national teams. I was never No. 1 in my age group in Queensland, but the family never suggested I give it away. And there's never been a hint of envy or jealousy. It is not the Rafter way to be like that. We've all achieved in different walks of life and my family has been integral to my success.

Steve, my oldest brother, is an accountant who handles all my business affairs. Geoff, along with my father, coached me and toured with me for a while. It was Geoff, in fact, who helped bankroll my career.

Peter travels with me more than anybody else these days and he's tremendous to have around. He takes care of a lot of hassles and shields me from unnecessary distractions. He's a good laugh and a really great bloke, just the kind of company I need more often than not.

My mother Jocelyn is my greatest supporter. If anybody wants the lowdown on my life, they should talk to Mum.

She did an interview once in which she said she knew her sixth baby — me — was going to be special. Mum went on to say she had chosen this particular diet, predicting she was going to produce a 'superbaby.' Mum maintains she knew a long time before anybody else that, in her words, 'Pat was going do something special.'

Needless to say the first US Open victory over Greg Rusedski was conclusive evidence for her that she was right all along.

I'll be working out in Bermuda this week getting ready for the Montreal tournament from Monday week and the road leading into the US Open. Before arriving home in Bermuda, I shot a couple of commercials, one for a telecommunications company, the other for a milk company.

Now it seems the entire international media wants an interview. Having arrived back in Bermuda, I agree to do a conference call through the ATP to celebrate reaching No. 1. I'm not sure how long I'm going to stay at the top of the mountain, but I can tell you the view is bloody good. It is just really exciting. I don't see being No. 1 as pressure. A few of the guys have struggled this year at the top. Kafelnikov is probably the best example of somebody who's worked really hard to get there and then fallen off a bit in terms of form and confidence.

I go into every tournament feeling the same sort of expectation and there is a degree of pressure attached to that. People want to beat you whether you are No. 2 or No. 1. If I am hitting the ball well, feeling confident, I am more than likely going to win. If I am not hitting the ball well, I am going to lose whether or not I am No. 1 or No. 50. It pretty much comes down to performing on the day.

I'm asked a lot about the importance I placed on the goal of reaching No. 1 and the truth is I never felt it was a realistic goal for me, so I never really focused on it. My goal is to do very well in the Grand Slams. It would be something to have the Davis Cup as well and the Super 9s; they are the main ones and the rest will take care of themselves.

On reflection, it's been a long and improbable road to No. 1. It doesn't seem that long ago I was hacking around on the Queensland satellite circuit, never suspecting I would reach this level. I remember as a kid having a junior coach who would make us say we were going to be No. 1 one day. It was his way of keeping tennis fun and building our confidence. But I could never yell it out. I just used to say it quietly or jokingly. I'm sure neither he nor I ever expected the ranking would come my way. I got a call from Lara today and she was a bit upset that she wouldn't be with me on the day I officially become No. 1. My brother Steve is leaving for Australia tomorrow, so I'll be on my own when the big day comes. I've got no problem with that. I told Lara I thought it was more appropriate that she was with me that night, rather than on Monday.

And on Monday when the fresh rankings list comes out, it will be time to get stuck into practice again. My body has recovered pretty well from the rigours of the Davis Cup and now it's time to get into some hard work again.

I'm not the type of person to look back. I try to learn from the past.

But having won a couple of Grand Slams and reached world No. 1, it's interesting to reflect on some of the turns my career has taken over the past couple of years.

I was asked the other day which match I considered to be the most important in my career. It's a tough question. You immediately think of the US Open finals against Rusedski and Flip, but one of the biggest of all my matches, I think, though not necessarily the best, was the semi-final in the US Open against Pete Sampras last year when I won in five sets.

The Canadian Open was a better match, but in the US Open semi-final against Pete, to get to my second consecutive final I had to play against the reigning Wimbledon champion, the bloke who had won the US Open four times and was desperate to win it again. That's why it was big.

The bonus from winning matches like that is what it teaches you about yourself. I used to lack confidence. I remember really getting down on myself over my losses and lack of form. You need to be tough on yourself to reach your potential, but now I've learned to temper it. Basically, if you're going to demand a lot from yourself, you have got to be balanced about it, too. There's no point in hammering yourself mentally for failing if you're not prepared to give yourself some credit for succeeding.

I probably have the same attitude that I had when I first started out on the Tour. Now that I have put two good years together — and I still believe I haven't done extraordinary things — what I find more now is that miracles happen. You simply have to give yourself an opportunity and then do your best to capitalise on it. That doesn't necessarily make me a great player, but I've certainly gained a lot of confidence.

I think I've become better at setting myself targets. I look at the schedule now and reflect on some of the things that have happened to me in my career and wonder, 'Can this happen?' and I say, 'Yeah, I think it can because of all the things that have happened so far.'

Incredibly, my feat in becoming No. 1 is being compared to the victory in the Tour de France of American Lance Armstrong, who has overcome cancer to win the greatest cycling race in the world. I'm not so sure it's a fair comparison. I am hearing more and more about it, even today, about what Lance has come through. He sounds like a remarkable person. Winning the Tour de France is just a huge thing for anyone, let alone someone who has been down on their luck health-wise.

The thing I want to avoid now is burnout: the day when I feel I can't look at a tennis racquet, let alone pick it up and go out to practise, or worse, play.

Those days come and go throughout the year for me. At times I feel that I have had enough of tennis; I really want to take a break for a while and generally I do. But if I don't, and I find myself losing on court, it actually gets me really fired up. It's amazing, but it seems that the more I lose, the more I fire up. The first two or three losses, I sort of handle, but if it becomes five or six or seven early losses, that is when I start picking up my game again and finding the strength to keep on. As bizarre as it sounds, in a way it helps me to lose matches.

So I really haven't suffered badly from mental burnout yet. I'm really fortunate. But if I felt flat over an extended period of time and the disappointment of losing wasn't kicking in to help me pick up again, then I would have to take a good break to recharge my batteries.

From what I understand, Tennis Australia has posted congratulatory advertisements in the Australian press. Even now — at 26 — I've been asked what might happen for me beyond tennis. Will I go on the seniors circuit? Will I coach some of the up-and-coming Aussie kids? As for the seniors circuit, I really don't know just yet. I don't know how much longer I am going to keep playing on the ATP Tour. It is becoming very tough. It is a long year, and I just wonder how much it can take out of me. But so far, I am still fit and healthy and I'll continue to play as long as I am enjoying myself. And after that, I will always try and help out the good young blokes and, more importantly, the guys who work hard and have a great attitude. I love working with Lleyton Hewitt — he's a terrific bloke.

He loves kicking my backside, but he is someone that I really respect as well. He's got a fantastic coach at the moment in Darren Cahill, so I might have to find somebody else. I just hope I can make a positive impact on everything that I do.

So much for the future.

Monday July 16 comes around and I become the 17th player in the world to hold the No. 1 ranking.

It's time to get stuck into the work of practising again. I am doing a little bit of work here in Bermuda and I feel quite good. The ball seems to be coming off the racquet okay. I will know after a few more days of practice how I am hitting it. I am going to get to Montreal next Thursday, so I will be there early to prepare. I won't play at least until Tuesday or Wednesday and I want to be ready to go. I am fairly sure my preparation will be pretty solid going into Montreal and I guess after that it depends on the draw and a bit of luck.

I want to do very well in this tournament. Obviously I did well last year in winning in Toronto, so my workload is picking up every day.

As I prepare to leave for the US mainland and eventually Canada, word comes of a storm brewing over some remarks I've made about Pete Sampras in the conference call. The other piece of news is that my reign at No. 1 might last less than a week.

Montreal to Indianapolis

FURORE

The interview I gave to the media a couple of days ago in celebration of reaching world No. 1 has come back to haunt me. Far from enjoying a couple of idyllic days on Bermuda, training and relaxing, the short break has turned into a nightmare.

Watching television in Pembroke, it quickly becomes obvious I'm now at the centre of a major controversy. If you believe the headlines, I hate Pete Sampras. Nothing could be further from the truth. Pete and I are rivals, we love to beat each other and, as humans, we are different.

So, for the benefit of those who weren't involved in the conference call, here are the questions and answers that led to a hysterical outpouring of stories about the so-called rift between Sampras and me.

Question: How do you see this rivalry going as far as it has with Sampras? He talks about wanting to get the No. 1 position back. You want to keep it. Do you see this as a turning point as far as the rivalry between you guys?

Patrick Rafter: It is always nice to beat Pete, whether it is on the court or in the rankings or in the Davis Cup. I get an incredible amount of enjoyment from being on top of him and just annoying him. We really can't be compared. I know we are in a whole different league and I am the first to respect that. I am looking forward to playing him again; hopefully having another couple of successful matches against him.

Question: Does the needle between you in recent times make your rise to No. 1 even more satisfying for you?

Patrick Rafter: Well, to be honest, it is just an achievement that I feel for myself. But if I know Pete is upset about it then it's even better.

Question: You mentioned your match with Pete in the semi-finals of the US Open. Did you feel that he tried to deny you some of the credit for the win when he had that slight injury? He didn't look too bad.

Patrick Rafter: Yeah, you never quite know with Pete. He seemed to have strained a thigh muscle but then he came out there and did some pretty extraordinary things. I really can't talk about how he was feeling. But every time he did move and move very quickly I was very annoyed. It was just very satisfying to win. Whether he was injured or not doesn't really worry me.

Question: Pat, you are such an easygoing guy. I just wonder what it is about Pete that riles you so much and how much did the antagonism or competition that you feel towards him help drive you towards being No. 1?

Patrick Rafter: Well, first I will answer the second question. He doesn't really bug me that much. Sometimes he makes certain comments that annoy me but it doesn't really drive me to be No. 1. It is something that I have always wanted to achieve regardless of the rivalry between us. But I think he says some really funny things at the wrong time. We are out there busting our guts and he tries to play down the reason why he lost, not showing a lot of respect to the other player, and that is what really upsets me about him and the reason why I try to piss him off as much as I can.

Question: A question about the tournament in Cincinnati last year and the way it ended. [I had been awarded the match on a line-call that Sampras didn't like.] I don't want to belabour this, but do you think that was the start of the thing between the two of you? Do you think that inspired you for the rest of the year to achieve what you have now?

Patrick Rafter: The Cincinnati situation was probably pretty well the start. I thought the match was so hard-fought and at a good level and it was put in the press a little bit negatively, which started to upset me. I thought it was uncalled for. But really he hasn't given me a huge inspiration for reaching No. 1 or winning other tournaments in my career, not at all. I have a lot of respect for him as one of the greatest players, but I really enjoy the rivalry that we have, whether I win or lose. I think it is pretty healthy for both of us.

My comments about Sampras were blown right out of proportion. I did not want him to feel badly about what I said. I don't hate the guy and I'm sure he doesn't hate me, either. Nor did I want to hurt him. It's not a war between Sampras and myself. We both love to win. That's what competition is all about, but it's not personal. My attitude towards him is simply that I love to beat him.

We're all out there busting our backsides every week and if I can find an edge to beat Pete, then I'll use it. Just as he would gladly do the same to me. Pete beat me eight or nine times in a row after I beat him the first time we played. I've won the last three and that's obviously something that annoys him.

Sure, there were some issues with Pete. There have been times when I've been disappointed with what Pete has had to say.

He's probably annoyed with some of the things I do and say.

I stand by what I said about him not giving his opponents sufficient respect because there are times when he loses and gives no credit to his opponent. That is an issue that irks me.

The media has had a lot of fun this week with my comments and I presume the ATP Tour is happy that it has got a good rivalry going. It certainly will make things interesting in the lead-in to the US Open. Sampras will be desperate to win the US Open for the fifth time and break the Grand Slam record of winning 13 singles titles.

I'll be going for three US Opens in a row and, if the rankings hold up, we'll be playing in the final. That's a long way off right now, but there's a pretty good chance I'll be bumping into Sampras over the next month.

The interview and the subsequent publicity about the way I supposedly felt about Pete has upset me and I want to talk to him. He says that he'd be happy to talk to me, so I've arranged to make contact with him in Los Angeles, Pete's home town. There's a tournament there this week and, if he wins it, Sampras will knock me out of the No. 1 position. While I'm hardly going to be wishing all the best in his quest to take away the ranking, I want to clear the air with him, but I won't be stepping back from anything I've said.

With the assistance of a few key people on the ATP Tour, Pete and I hookup by telephone and, afterwards, I'm happy to report the 'war' between Sampras and myself is over.

The truth is that it never existed. I was eager to telephone Pete this week. I've now had the opportunity to read most of the articles and, in the main, they were fine. Some of the headlines, however, tended to exaggerate the situation.

Sampras was very receptive. I called him in California at an appropriate time and we had a good chat. I stood by some of the things I had said about Pete and he apologised for anything that he might have said which upset me. He couldn't have been more accommodating.

I was concerned that Sampras might have been unfairly hurt by some of the things attributed to me. The last thing I wanted was for him to be hurt by a misinterpretation.

It quickly became obvious that there had been a fair bit of confusion. I feel we have opened up the lines of communication and I can't see a problem developing again.

Sampras, meanwhile, continues to make strong inroads in LA. I've decided to bypass the tournament this year and hopefully be ready for Montreal, site of the Canadian Open.

There's a lot riding on the LA tournament and, as fate would have it, there's a rematch of the Wimbledon final: Sampras v Agassi. Sampras produces wonderful tennis to win his third tournament in a row.

The No. 1 ranking is deservedly his. I must say I would have preferred to have had a bit more time to hang on to it. Hopefully it will be mine again soon. If I can retain the Canadian Open title in Montreal then I will go some way towards that goal.

For the moment, I just want to get back on court, win some matches and find my name in the media for all the right reasons.

My first match is against Alex O'Brien, who was on the American team in Boston. I was really pleased with my form. I won 6–0 6–2 in 45 minutes, so I couldn't complain. I was also happy with my 6–3 6–4 win over Jiri Novak. I served okay, but because my right shoulder is still giving me trouble, I'm concerned that I won't be able to maintain the consistency. The tendinitis is not too bad at the moment and it's alright once I get warm. I tend to feel it when I've cooled down and when I go to bed.

Unfortunately I can't maintain the momentum and, for the third time this year, I lose to Nicolas Kiefer. I can't say it's a record that I particularly like, but I've yet to play good tennis against Nicolas.

On a brighter note, Jonas and I catch up for our first doubles tournament together since Wimbledon. I'd committed to this event a while back and, after the dramas in England, it's a great feeling to pull off the doubles title.

From Montreal, we head south for Cincinnati and the Greater American Insurance ATP Championships. I won this event last year, beating Pete Sampras in the final, and I would love to repeat the effort. My shoulder is obviously a concern and I've started a course of anti-inflammatories to counter the pain. Now that I'm on medication for the shoulder, it's holding up really well. So far, so good. We have a long summer to go, so I'm trying to keep a check on it.

After beating Daniel Vacek 7–6 (7–3) 6–3, my next match is against Nicolas Lapentti. If I get through Lapentti, I'll probably bump into Michael Chang, a great competitor who's been in the wars for a while now.

As it turns out, I play one of my best matches in ages in getting over Lapentti. The Chang match could not have panned out any better, either. I was really on top of my game and everything worked perfectly. Usually I'm not that aggressive on my forehand, but today it worked. The score is 6–2 6–1.

The semi-finals are a promoter's dream. For the first time since Wimbledon in 1993, the tournament has delivered the top four seeds into the semi-finals. Pete Sampras will play Agassi and I've got Yevgeny Kafelnikov. The Kafelnikov match works out perfectly, another straight-sets victory, this time 6–4 6–2. Pete beats Andre, so I decide to have a bit of fun with the media. I tell them there will be no love lost in the final.

This, predictably, has been billed as a grudge match. It is nothing of the sort, of course, but it is true to say we're both eager to win. It ends up being Pete's day. He beats me 7–6 (9–7) 6–3 and, worse, I do my shoulder again. Where this leaves me for the US Open, I'm not really sure. I'm not going to use the injury as an excuse or anything. I noticed it halfway through the tiebreaker, but it didn't affect my serve. I think I jarred it trying to return Sampras's serve.

At the end of the match, Pete and I shared a private moment in public, if that doesn't sound too much like a contradiction. It was a very nice conversation. Pete was complimentary, something along the lines of, 'Well done. I really enjoyed the match. I just hope we can have some more fun next time.' I said well done and good luck for the rest of the summer.

It's off to the RCA Championships in Indianapolis. Unfortunately, after reaching the quarter-finals, despite severe pain in my shoulder, I am advised by the tournament trainer and a team of doctors to withdraw. They also advise me to seriously consider not playing in Long Island next week, which means I won't play another match until the US Open begins in 10 days. Pete Sampras also suffers a setback. He damages a hip flexor when playing Vince Spadea and has to retire from their quarter-final with the score at a set-all. Between us, we've won the past four US Open titles and now we're both injured with less than two weeks to go to the Open. I head back to Bermuda to freshen up. Although I'm a bit sore right now, I'm confident I will be okay for the last Slam of the year.

US OPEN

Centre court in the Arthur Ashe Stadium is not exactly as I remember it. I've just come from a practice session with Lleyton Hewitt on an outside court and I'm confronted by the sight of Martina Hingis, Serena Williams, Andre Agassi and Pete Sampras drilling balls at plastic targets.

The targets are being used to raise money for the Arthur Ashe Foundation. Arthur was one of the greatest champions tennis has known. He died in 1993 from AIDS, which he contracted during a blood transfusion when he was having open-heart surgery. Arthur fought for much of his life against racism — he was one of the few black athletes to break into top-flight tennis — and his premature death affected a lot of people because of the wide range of humanitarian causes he had become involved with.

Having learned of Arthur's determination to help others, everybody wants to lend their support to the foundation. That's how a group of us ended up on centre court, serving balls at the stationary targets. Every time we hit a board, the cash figure on the target was added to a rapidly growing target. With Andre and Martina firing incredibly accurate groundstrokes, we helped raise quite a bit of money.

It is now only two days to the start of the Open. My shoulder feels better and I've had a couple of practice sessions today against Lleyton, who appears to have gotten over his ankle injury.

Both times there were heaps of people around. The really encouraging thing was the number of kids hanging around for autographs.

The USTA has poured a lot of money into redeveloping Flushing Meadows over the past couple of years and they have now developed a world-class facility.

It wasn't that long ago that Kevin Curren, who played in the 1985 Wimbledon final, said this place ought to be blown up. Over the years I'm sure a succession of players would have agreed with him as they played in substandard conditions, often made worse by low-flying aircraft taking off and landing at nearby La Guardia Airport. New York's mayor Rudolph Giuliani has since struck a deal with the aviation authorities to have the flight paths diverted whenever possible. The difference, coupled with the upgraded facilities, has been profound.

While tennis is the main theme on what is pretty much a fun day at Flushing Meadows, there is music and a lot of activities for the kids as well. Singer Britney Spears made a cameo appearance on a temporary stage before we got to go out on court and fire off a few serves.

After returning to the locker-room, Lleyton and I head out for another practice session. The shoulder is feeling better and better all the time. Two days out from the start of the tournament, I think my shoulder is feeling about 95 per cent.

After finishing practice, getting a little more treatment and heading back to the hotel for a meal, it's time to kick back and relax a bit. The next fortnight — I'm hoping I'm still going to be in the running for that long — is going to be tough on the mind and body, so it's important to rest.

Unfortunately for Mark Philippoussis, his US Open is over before it starts. The knee he injured at Wimbledon in July still hasn't recovered and he's decided to withdraw. It's a smart move, even though it would have been a tough decision, given how well he went at Flushing Meadows last year.

But the reality is that he's got to take a long-range view and think of the future. He has a lot of rankings points to defend here, but the most important thing is his health. By the time Mark contacted the referee's office to officially withdraw, not too many people were surprised.

No-one had seen Flip out practising and we all knew the knee and his left ankle were swollen. His absence will definitely weaken the Australian presence, but we've still got plenty of blokes who can give the title a really good shot.

The weather is perfect, warm without being hot. Sunday is much the same. The nerves are starting to come into play a bit now. I organise a practice session with Dutchman John Van Lottum. He hits the ball very well. It's important to vary your practice partners as much as you can.

When we got back to the locker-room, the place was abuzz over an injury to Pete Sampras. He limped back into the locker-room after hurting his back in practice.

No-one seems to know just how dire the injury is. The official line from the tournament doctor is that Pete needs to rest the back before he plays Russian teenager Marat Safin, who earlier in the day won the MFS Pro Championships in Boston, defeating Greg Rusedski in the final.

I've been given Monday off. I plan to come back out to Flushing Meadows, which sits across the railway tracks from Shea Stadium — home to the New York Mets baseball team — for a midday practice session.

The first day passes without incident. Andre Agassi, Carlos Moya, Marcelo Rios and Yevgeny Kafelnikov, all former world No. 1 players, reach the second round, but the truly inspirational performance is that of Scotty Draper out on court seven.

This was Scott's first appearance at a Grand Slam since the death of his wife Kellie back on July 19. Most of the boys went out to watch the match which, unfortunately, didn't last long as Paul Goldstein won 6–3 6–1 6–0.

Scott has been fantastic in the wake of Kel's death and the only reason he's playing right now is to try and get some kind of balance back into his life. He simply wasn't switched on mentally for the match but, in the circumstances, who would be?

You could tell from watching Goldstein that he felt really uncomfortable taking points off Scotty. I can only imagine the depth of Scott's pain right now. Tennis must seem irrelevant, but he's out there trying to rebuild his life.

He's always had a lot of respect from all the players on the Tour and, for those who watched the way he conducted himself today, there was even more reason to admire the guy. Scotty was one of three Australians to lose on the first day. The others were his good friend Lisa McShea, who went out to watch him play before her own match, and Jelena Dokic, who was beaten on centre court by Arantxa Sanchez Vicario, who won the women's title here in 1994.

Another Queenslander, Nicole Pratt, kept the Aussie flag flying with a good straight-sets win.

A record single-session crowd of 27 809 came through the gates today, which effectively shoots down the argument that tennis is wallowing in the US.

I don't know where some of these theories come from. It was only a few years ago that we had to contend with the 'tennis is dying' accusations. From where I sit, the women's game could not be in better shape and the men's game is the healthiest it's been for a long time.

The US is a tough market, especially in the summer when baseball is huge. The football season is now just starting, so tennis has plenty of competition. Andre Agassi, Pete Sampras and the Williams sisters, Venus and Serena, along with Lindsay Davenport have been great for lifting the profile of the game in the US. The Davis Cup tie between Australia and the Americans sold out in a matter of minutes when the tickets were released, so the bad-news theories just don't equate with the facts.

The order of play for the second day comes out late in the afternoon. I've been given the night match on centre court.

After getting more treatment from Andrea, I came out to the courts at about six to warm up with Paul Kilderry. I'm feeling great. The shoulder is holding up well and I'm looking forward to competing against Cedric Pioline, who's a good mate.

Serena Williams and Kimberley Po are due to play the first match of the night session and it's important to keep an eye on the progress of that match while preparing in the locker-room. The player lounge and locker-room at Flushing Meadows are now world-class.

There's a few nerves as Williams makes short work of Po. An official from the referee's offices comes into the locker-room to tell Cedric and me that's it's time to play. The last time I walked down this corridor to play a match here was in last year's final.

That match with Mark Philippoussis seems a long time ago now and how circumstances have changed. My goal is to start well and get on top of Pioline. That's the type of approach that's worked for me in the past.

There's an amazing atmosphere at night at Flushing Meadows. Centre court holds about 22 000 people and it's an arena that has a great feel.

I've got Lara, my brothers Steve and Pete, Newk, Rochey, Muddy, Kilderry and Andrea sitting in my support box and there are pockets of Australians in the Tuesday-night crowd. The structure of the complex means that most of the paying customers are sitting higher up in the stands. The corporate crowd is on the concourse level. Among the notables here tonight is businessman Donald Trump. Donald and his friends turned up to my party after the US Open last year. I'm hoping there will be a similar cause for celebration at the end of this tournament. Miss Universe is looking on — it turns out she's barracking for Cedric. Actors Paul Newman and his wife Joanne Woodward are also in attendance, along with Andrea Jaeger, the former women's world No. 2.

The match started perfectly for me. I broke Pioline's serve in the first game of the match and everything was going along smoothly and then my shoulder began to give me problems.

I felt a sharp pain when serving. As the match wore on, I began to feel it more and more, particularly when I tried to make a backhand return off some of Cedric's heavier serves. I knew I was in trouble but, at that stage, I was hoping some treatment at the change of ends might alleviate the problem.

The really scary thing was that, with all the work Andrea had put into the shoulder, I had felt great coming in. Now, with the match only five games old, I was starting to struggle. I looked across at Alex Stober, a German physiotherapist who works on the ATP Tour as a trainer. I knew I had to get some help as soon as I could, even though I was playing well and felt I had control of the match, if not the state of my shoulder.

I wasn't serving at full power because of the pain I was feeling, but I was hitting the lines and coming up with good serves when I needed them — which was pretty often.

With the score at 5–4, I got to 30–0 pretty comfortably and then lost the next three points. I was down a break point and decided to gamble. Fortunately for me, it came off with a big ace down the middle. But on the next point, I fell on my right shoulder as I tried to make a volley of a stinging Pioline return.

The amazing thing was that the fall didn't cause me any problems and I served out the set, but I was now pretty desperate to get Alex out there to work on the shoulder.

Under the rules, players are not allowed to have treatment on successive changes of ends, but you can do it every second change. In all, Alex came out to see me five times. With Alex coming out so often, Cedric began to become a little concerned about the rules. He asked the tournament supervisor Bill Gilmour for a ruling and was told my actions were legal.

The second set went pretty smoothly. I broke serve in the ninth game when Pioline dragged a backhand wide and then went up by two-sets-to-love by winning the following game — but it had been a big struggle.

Pioline was beginning to nail my serve and the pain wasn't going away. I knew then and there, no matter whether I won or lost, that I wouldn't be able to play my second-round match. By now, I was only able to serve flat.

I couldn't get my kick-serve to work and that shot has basically been the secret of my success here, where the ball bounces high and gives me time to get into the net to play volleys. In my previous matches in Montreal and Indianapolis, I was able to get away with serving flat because the shoulder wasn't getting any worse.

But now, the pain was terrible.

Pioline is too good a player not to take advantage and he began to break down my game. I dropped serve in the fourth game of the third set after Cedric drilled a fantastic backhand pass down the line.

I got some more treatment at the end of the third set and my only hope now was to win the fourth set. Although I was dubious about being able to continue in the tournament beyond the first round, I definitely didn't want to walk off as a loser having won the past two titles.

Pioline broke my serve again in the third game before I levelled the score in the following game. Cedric started to get a little tight and, in the 10th game, served three double faults, but I still couldn't take advantage.

By now, I was really in trouble.

With the score at 5–5, the pressure was starting to build. I double-faulted before Pioline made another winning backhand pass. At 30–40, I put a backhand volley into the net and the match was as good as dead as Pioline levelled the match at two sets all.

I knew I was finished, but I couldn't retire at that stage. I sat there at the following change of ends, knowing I should have just walked straight off, but I couldn't bring myself to do it. It was very tough to even consider it. Especially on that court, at this event. My form had been pretty good coming into this tournament, despite the injury. I had been feeling pretty confident about having some good wins and I knew I was now going to struggle to complete this match, let alone win it.

I felt terrible sitting there. I had just lost my serve and Pioline was starting to get pumped up. Because we're mates, I didn't want him to be upset with me if I retired. I've never used injury as an excuse and I didn't want to start now.

As I went out for the first game of the fifth set, I was already wondering what the hell I was doing out there. There was no point. I missed two backhand volleys, Cedric came in and made a volley winner and then I hit a forehand into the net.

As I walked back towards my courtside chair for the change of ends, I stopped under the umpire's chair and beckoned Cedric over to the net. It was an awkward moment for me because I didn't know what to say.

There were a lot of emotions running through me, but I didn't want to take anything away from Pioline. I told him I was sorry. I remember saying, 'I probably shouldn't continue here. I don't really know why I am. I've had enough of this, but I don't want to take away any of the glory or the victory.'

I didn't want Cedric to think I was denying any of that because he deserved it. He was fine about it. I'm sure he felt bad for me, even though, as he said later, a win is a win. After briefly burying my head in a towel and packing my bags, I walked off — and was booed.

There were obviously a few guys who'd had a few beers, but I certainly didn't expect some of the crowd to react the way they did. It was very sad. But what could I do? I've played here the past two years and I always had a really good reception.

To be booed off after having to retire with the shoulder problem hurt, there's no doubt about it. But in New York, where they can't get enough of you if you're winning, they can obviously turn on you quickly if they see you as a loser. I remember walking off court at the Australian Open in

1996 after hurting my wrist against Mauricio Hadad and being jeered by a few people, but this was much worse.

It was an upsetting and strange way to leave the tournament. I have had so many good moments at the US Open, and hopefully there will be a lot more in the future, and I don't often leave like this.

It is a disappointing outcome, but I knew it was coming. I was preparing myself for it, while at the same time hoping to find a miracle to avoid it.

The press conference didn't take long before we took a car back into Manhattan to consider the future. The last time I made this trip after playing at the US Open, I was in a much different frame of mind. After getting back to the hotel, a group of about 10 or 15 of us wandered across the road to a little deli and just sat around having a few beers with some pizza. It was a pretty casual night. We talked about what had happened and what to do next.

I've already made up my mind to have a number of scans on the shoulder and I'll also consult a couple of specialists for their opinions. I'm anxious to avoid surgery. I've always been dismissive of it unless it's a last resort. But I have to be sensible. If the scans show I need surgery, I'll do it.

The first appointment is soon after midday with Dr David Altchek, who runs a scan on the shoulder. The scan shows I've got a small tear of the rotator cuff in the right shoulder. Altchek recommends rest and therapy and we begin immediately.

A lot of tennis players have had rotator cuff problems over the years and the severity of the injury varies from extreme to minor. In some cases, it has meant the end of some careers.

Dr Altchek assures me that I'm not in that position. With Andrea, we sit down to work out a rehabilitation program. As ridiculous as it seems, I've still got a chance to play in the Davis Cup semi-final against Russia in just over three weeks. If I was scheduled to play another tournament then, there's no way I would even consider it. But this is Davis Cup and it means the world to me.

Andrea reckons that we'll know within a week if I'll be able to recover. I lift some weights in the gym just to test the strength in the shoulder and there's not much there.

Watching the US Open from the hotel room seems a little strange compared to the past two years. But there's no way I want to go out to the courts. I'm content to lay low and take in a bit of New York.

Friday night turns out to be one of the most relaxing nights I've had in ages. A big group of us — about 30 or 35 — went down to Soho for dinner. We had a great meal and finished up pretty late.

The injuries keep coming at the Open. Carlos Moya has broken down with a back injury and is unsure of his program for the rest of the year.

With the final major of the year still to reach the halfway point, Sampras, Moya and myself have all been forced out with injuries. Greg Rusedski, who missed five weeks with a foot problem, has called for a two-month break at the end of each season and there's a lot of merit in what he says.

If you consider that the Davis Cup does not finish until the first week of December and the Australian summer circuit starts basically from New Year's Day, there is virtually no time to rest — unless you're injured and attempting to recover.

It would be great if the schedule wasn't as busy, but it's just the way it is. Every country seems to want to have their own tournament and some nations have several events, which means a lot of travel for the players.

Everyone is in the same boat and I know the ATP Tour is actively buying back tournaments from private owners so that the schedule is structured in a better way.

Newk and Rochey have organised a meeting of the Davis Cup players to work out a way of approaching the semi-final tie in Brisbane in three weeks. We've got to come up with a way of getting through this situation with all the injuries.

I desperately want to give myself a chance, no matter how slim, of making it to the court in Brisbane. I'll be there one way or the other. Playing in the Davis Cup at home has been a dream of mine for a long time.

The events of Tuesday night continue to swirl around in my mind. It was such a strange way for it all to end. I felt sorry for Cedric that the match finished as it did.

My half of the draw is now wide open. 'What ifs' don't count for much in tennis, but it's impossible not to wonder about what might have been. The reality is that I'm out of the tournament and that a new name will go on the trophy this year.

All is not lost for the Aussie campaign, though. Richard Fromberg, Lleyton Hewitt and Wayne Arthurs are playing really well.

With the rain from Tropical Storm Dennis hitting New York, Sunday provides the opportunity to get more treatment, while out at the tennis, Yevgeny Kafelnikov predicts that only three players can win this year's tournament. He nominates himself, Andre Agassi and Richard Krajicek. It seems Kafelnikov was of that opinion even before Pete, myself and Mark Philippoussis pulled out.

I would have loved to have proved him wrong. I guess we'll never know.

The rest of my time in New York is taken up with getting treatment on the shoulder and relaxing with Lara. We've seen a couple of shows, including *Dr Jekyll and Mr Hyde* and the Umbilical Brothers.

As good as it has been — New York is a great town — I would have preferred to have been out on the courts. It's not to be. The doctors tell me I'm out for at least six or eight weeks, which means I'll miss the Davis Cup tie in Brisbane as well.

The only way I'll play again this year is if Australia can win the semi-final. If that happens, I'll try and play a couple of tournaments late in the year to get ready to help out in the final in December.

I'm heading back to Australia tonight as the injury list at the Open hits nine with Magnus Norman retiring because of a back injury. Cedric Pioline has reached the semi-finals against another longstanding rival of mine, Todd Martin. Kafelnikov and Agassi are in the other semi-final. It's interesting, but pointless, to ponder what might have been.

Serena Williams wins the singles title over Martina Hingis, who had beaten Serena's big sister Venus in the semi-finals. The Williams girls then combine to win the women's doubles. I think they're fantastic for the sport. Todd beats Cedric pretty easily in their semi-final, while Andre gets past Kafelnikov in four sets. I would have loved to have been there. Andre beat me in the Wimbledon semis, but I'd beaten him in Rome. This is his best surface and he would have started favourite against just about anybody, except for an in-form and fit Sampras.

Watching the final from Australia is a little strange. It's only 12 months since I was there and less than two weeks ago I was still in the tournament. Now I'm sitting back in Australia. Andre completes a fabulous year at the Grand Slams by winning a great five-set final against Todd after Todd had led by two sets to one. He played Andre exactly the way you have to if you want to win, but couldn't quite pull it off.

Andre is clearly the best player in the world right now and he has the results to prove it. I can relate to the satisfaction and the joy he felt as he lifted up the trophy at the victory presentation. It is an incredible feeling. Hopefully I can experience it again at one of the majors in 2000, maybe at the Australian Open or Wimbledon.

Other books by HarperSports

THE HARD WAY
ROBBIE SLATER WITH MATTHEW HALL

Robbie Slater was the heart and soul of the Socceroos for over a decade of international football and the first Australian player to win a Championship medal in the English Premier League.

From his junior days playing backyard cricket with Steve and Mark Waugh in the suburbs of Sydney to sharing the field with Diego Maradona in Buenos Aires's River Plate Stadium, Slater made the most of his humble beginnings. His fighting spirit, on-the-ball skills and superb fitness saw him play close to forty internationals for his country and forge a distinguished career in Europe for clubs such as Lens, Blackburn Rovers, West Ham United and Southampton alongside and against some of the greats of modern football: Alan Shearer, Eric Cantona, Jean-Pierre Papin, Ryan Giggs, Mark Bosnich, Zinedine Zidane, Dennis Bergkamp. But with the glory came the pain: Australia's heartbreaking exit from the 1998 World Cup qualifiers at the hands of Iran shattered his long-held dream of playing on football's ultimate stage.

Now playing in Australia, Slater is captain and leading light of National Soccer League superclub Northern Spirit.

With a candour and refreshingly humorous style not found in most sports autobiographies, *The Hard Way* is the most explosive sports book of the year.

ISBN 0 7322 6483 9

EVERYONE AND PHAR LAP
PETER FITZSIMONS

Peter FitzSimons has been described as Australia's favourite sports writer. His first collection of sports writing, *Everyone but Phar Lap*, was a national bestseller, and his columns in the *Sydney Morning Herald* are a must-read for all sports fans. Now he's done it again. *Everyone and Phar Lap* is another humorous, insightful and engaging collection of what FitzSimons called 'sportraits', profiles of our sporting greats.

As Australia primes itself for the first Olympic Games of the new millennium, FitzSimons turns his razor-sharp sights on a veritable who's who of sporting heroes from the last 150 years and others who will seize our hearts and imaginations in the years to come: from Victor Trumper, Sir Donald Bradman, Roy Cazaly, Phar Lap and Mark Edmondson to John Bertrand, Duncan Armstrong, Ian Roberts, Zoe Goss, Shane Warne and Heather Turland.

If you have ever cheered an Aussie home, or shed a tear after an Australian victory or defeat, *Everyone and Phar Lap* is for you.

ISBN 0 7322 6730 7